What others say about

Falling to Heaven

"Mickey Robinson's story is ... one of the most engaging stories you are likely ... ... sizzles
with supernatural encounter. ... matter where you may be on
your spiritual journey, the message in these pages will bring
you face to face with a God of infinite love and compassion."

Steve Fry
President, Messenger Fellowship
Senior Pastor, Belmont Church

"Falling to Heaven is a gripping message about a man who
flew into the fires of destruction, only for them to be changed
into the flames of transforming love. From a body caught in a
raging fire, fashioned into a heart that will capture you, it will
grip your entire being. As you read—watch out—it just might
light a fire in you!"

Jim W. Goll
Ministry to the Nations
International Author and Speaker

"Mickey's life has transcended the outer reaches of tragedy
and triumph. His story will encourage and give hope to everyone who reads it. It is a 'must read' for those who have
reached the end of their own resources."

Thomas S. Caldwell
Chairman, Caldwell Securities Ltd.
Toronto, Canada

Falling
to Heaven

by Mickey Robinson

FALLING TO HEAVEN

Co-Published by:
Arrow Publications
P.O. Box 10102
Cedar Rapids, IA 52410
Phone: (319) 395-7833
Toll Free: (877) 363-6889
Fax: (319) 395-7353
Web Site: http://www.frangipane.org

Dedicated to

my children,

Michael,

Matthew,

Jacob,

Elizabeth,

you are my treasures,

and to Barbara,

a braver woman,

deeper vessel,

truer beauty,

I cannot imagine.

Table of Contents

foreword

We all wonder at times about life after death. On our bed late at night, or perhaps upon hearing of the sudden death of a friend, with fear we look up into the vast unknown and ponder, "Is there a God? Are there literal places called heaven and hell?"

We fear death because we do not have answers. Without becoming theological, Mickey Robinson answers many of our questions about the afterlife and, perhaps more importantly, he points us to the Lord, our eternal helper in this present life.

Mickey lets us know that life has many unexplainable injustices, but there is a God who can help us through anything. Mickey's experience with Jesus Christ will touch your heart.

I love Mickey Robinson. He is probably the most unique person I know, and his testimony is probably the most powerful.

Francis Frangipane
Senior Minister, River of Life Ministries
Author and International Speaker

Acknowledgements

If I were to attempt to thank all those who have helped me on this journey, it would resemble a telephone book! However, I would be remiss not to honor those who have made it possible to publish this humble story.

Chloe Lovejoy, more than a writer, you are a master storyteller and a most trusted friend. "God sits in the heavens and laughs"—by putting us together He created the perfect sitcom. You are a woman of tender vision and great gifting, for just such a time as this. Thanks for loving our family so much.

Sandy Terrano, www.yellowhouse.com, for your fantastic cover art.

Lila Nelson, for your patient editorial skill and sound wisdom.

Anahid Schweikert, for writing such a concise, yet comprehensive article, and for your advice.

Anne Severance, for your constant love and encouragement, and critical help in wrapping up the epilogue.

Thank you so much, Francis and Denise Frangipane, for the many years of inspiration that are only overshadowed by your unwavering love and desire to see our family be blessed and prosper.

To Mahesh and Bonnie Chavda, for your friendship, loyalty, and your stellar example of honoring God above all. It shall always be one of our greatest treasures.

To James and Michal Ann Goll, for the pleasure it has been for us to partner with you on so many levels. However, the connection we have as we share our lives is a joy and a tremendous blessing, not to mention the fun!

Thanks to Tom and Dorothy Caldwell, and Caldwell Securities, for your faithful support and wise counsel.

To Phil Keaggy, for being my oldest friend in the Lord and the first person to ever share His love with me.

To Dennis and Susan Freeman, our dear comrades, for true friendship—more solid than the rock on the Georgian Bay. May God complete His plans in our lives together.

To Robert Robinson, thank you, my brother, for sacrificially giving of your time and strength to care for me in the hospital and at home in those early years. May God richly reward you!

Posthumous thanks to my mother, Jean Robinson, for never giving up . . . even when everyone told you I would die. Your perseverance has been inherited by all of us.

As well, thank you to Dan Harding, for courageously risking your life to save mine, and for tough love to make me get up and get going. Only the Lord could ever know where that would eventually lead.

Most of all, thanks to my precious family. My dear wife and life partner, Barbara, and our beautiful children, Michael, Matthew, Jacob and Elizabeth, who absolutely define the amazing reality of being our treasured gifts from the Lord.

To Jesus, my Lord and Savior. You have worked all these wonders. To You be all thanksgiving.

Introduction

This book is a story about life—life seen through the eyes of a young man born in the last half of the twentieth century. In this half century, more change has taken place than in all previous history added together. The population has more than doubled. Technology, information and knowledge increases and is shared globally, as it happens! The post-World War II society in America emerged—lavishly filled with freedom, prosperity, and unprecedented opportunity and power.

The ascent to achieve the American dream was dangled before this young man's eyes and mind, glamorously portrayed by TV, movies, music, sports, and a handsome young American president. This brave new society also contained dark, ominous shadows of the Cold War, potential nuclear annihilation, and the breakdown of some sound traditional values. The revolutionary aspect of the turbulent late '60s trumpeted free love, drugs, lawlessness, and "God is dead" or "God is—" whatever you want your god to be.

The young man this story is about grew up in the ideal American suburban middle to upper class dream. Even his home street address, Pleasant Valley, gave the impression of near utopian, mid-American optimism.

However, his home life was plagued with family strife, alcoholism, and unpleasant disharmony. These conditions were not uncommon in that era—just more hidden than in the present era.

Looking outside his family role models, he gravitated to a lifestyle of adventurous, "live for the moment" pleasure seeking, until his world was savagely interrupted by a tragic collision with human mortality.

At a point of utter hopelessness, he passed from this natural world into the Spirit realm. He was sent back to be a messenger, a messenger of life and hope to all people. "He slipped the surly bonds of earth and touched the face of God."

I am that young man. This is my story.

Mickey Robinson, 2003

Chapter One

Prologue: Kiss the Sky

August 15, 1968

The walls of the factory glowed in the sweltering heat of summer. As humidity turned the Otis Elevator warehouse into a steam bath, workers moved like ants in a puddle of molasses.

Everyone, that is, except me.

I was nineteen years old, and not even eight hours of hard work could slow me down. I just put my body in gear until the four o'clock whistle blew, then launched out of that warehouse like a heat-seeking missile.

Turning the key on my '63 Ford, I heard a voice behind me.

"Hey, Mickey, you want to get a beer?"

"No. I have to get to the airfield," I said. "Another time, maybe."

I didn't look to see who was talking before switching on the radio and grabbing a cigarette. As the squeal of an electric guitar pierced the air, I sped out of the parking lot and headed for the back road home.

"Lookin' for adventure, and whatever comes our way." The Ohio countryside became a green blur as the speedometer hit 90.

"Yeah, gotta go, make it happen . . ." The road stretched before me like a magic carpet, as I caught my reflection in the rearview mirror. I was a good-looking kid with places to go and people to see. My high school teacher said the world

was just waiting for me, but just then I didn't care about the world.

I was in love with the sky.

Just five months before, I'd jumped out of an airplane for the very first time and floated to earth beneath an old olive-drab parachute. That jump was hardly spectacular, yet something amazing happened when I stepped into the sky that day. An unseen hand punched a delete button in my soul. From that moment on, everything in my life disappeared except the desire for more. More sky, more sensation, more speed.

Hurtling through ozone-drenched atmosphere at 125 mph filled me with more life and freedom than I'd ever known. *Free falling* was the right name for my new craving; I was passionately falling into freedom! In those elongated seconds before my chute opened, there was no past and no future. No draft number. No time clock. No boredom. No boundaries. If I could have injected free falling into my veins, I would have done it without a moment's hesitation.

As I pulled into the driveway, my thoughts were still consumed with this new love of my life. I took one last drag before flicking the cigarette over my shoulder. Standing on the front porch was my fourteen-year-old brother, impatiently waiting for me with my packed parachute at his feet.

Leaving the radio playing full-blast, I wordlessly bound up the steps and brushed past him through the front door.

As soon as I entered the bedroom, I peeled off my khaki uniform and climbed into the clean, white jumpsuit that smelled of sky. As I grabbed my boots and started back down the hall, I caught a glimpse of my mother in the kitchen. She didn't turn around and I didn't stop. She knew I was in a hurry. I was always in a hurry.

My brother and I threw the gear in the trunk and took off for the airfield in a cloud of dust. As the speedometer climbed, I turned to him and said, "So . . . now you're grounded."

"Don't rub it in," he said with a pained look on his face. "How'd you like to be stuck down here?"

"Don't sweat it," I said. "You've got all the time in the world to fly."

My brother loved the sport as much as I did, but he was under-age. Just a few days before, an air traffic controller had gotten wise to his jumping and put his skydiving career on hold.

As we pulled into the Brunswick Flying Ranch, I spotted the Piper Cherokee Six all gassed and ready to go. Although this wasn't much of an airport, it was convenient for me. A 2,200-ft runway and a plane was all I needed to support my habit.

Walking from my car to the runway, I could feel all eyes on me. I liked that feeling. At the factory I was just a name on a timecard, but here I belonged to a tribe of elite beings. People wanted to get close to me, hoping to catch courage the way beggars catch coins from a rich man passing by.

In every sport, people gravitate toward the guy who has the goods. Well, I had the goods for skydiving. And I knew it.

"Hey, Superstar!"

I looked up into the grinning face of my hero and mentor, Dan. One of the first Americans to become a licensed sky-diver after World War II, Dan was a living legend in a sport now being taken over by thrill-seekers and adrenaline junk-ies.

He'd recently initiated me into the mysteries of *relative work,* the highly synchronized maneuvers where skydivers join together at corresponding speeds. Tonight Dan, Steve and I were planning to jump at 13,500 feet and link together for a 66-second free fall.

Also joining us for this short flight would be two student jumpers. Our pilot, Walt, planned to let the first student out at 2,500 feet and then go on up to 4,000 feet so the other guy could make a ten-second free fall.

All six of us were looking forward to trying out Walt's new aircraft. This Cherokee Six promised to be excellent for skydiving, with plenty of power so we could get up to jump altitude quickly.

The farmland of Ohio spread around us like a golden quilt as we gathered in the shadow of the plane that hot August evening. As I breathed in the rich smell of summer hay, the falling sun set the earth ablaze with color.

Just then Walt signaled that it was time to go.

He'd removed all except the pilot's seat from the plane, so there was room enough for all five skydivers and our equipment. As we climbed into the aircraft one at a time, I grabbed a place on the floor toward the back. I was just getting settled when I heard Steve call my name.

"Hey, Mickey, switch with me, will you? I have to go first, and it'll be a drag climbing over you."

I quickly moved forward to a spot on the floor beside Walt, who was now flipping switches and doing pre-flight checks. Finally he pulled back on the throttle and we started a slow roll down the runway. Spotting my brother's forlorn face in the crowd, I gave him a grinning thumbs-up as the plane cruised by him like a convertible in a parade.

Then I thought I heard a strange noise. Was the engine sputtering slightly, or was it my imagination?

I listened again. The engine was purring loudly. I must have been mistaken. Settling back-to-back against another skydiver and resting my head against the fuselage, I closed my eyes. It would be awhile before we reached 13,500 feet, so I decided to take a little nap. I was never nervous before a jump. The closer I got to the actual moment, the more relaxed I became.

The drone of the engine and extreme summer heat lulled me into a twilight sleep almost immediately. Then I suddenly remembered something that had happened a few days before when I'd gone to visit an old friend at the hospital.

I hated hospitals. They were dreary places full of sick people, and I couldn't wait to get out of there. But as I was leaving, I passed an old man slowly making his way down the hall. "Young man!" he called out in a thick Middle Eastern accent. I stopped and hesitantly turned around.

"You're a good-looking boy!"

"Thank you," I stammered, a little embarrassed.

"You have such nice skin!"

Without another word, he turned and continued tottering down the hall. I smiled and stole a glance at my forearm. Yeah, I did have a nice tan. It was summer and I looked pretty good.

Suddenly I was jolted awake as Walt pulled the throttle wide open for takeoff. My body leaned like a sack of cement into the back of the other skydiver. I shook my head a few times to clear away the memory of that old man. Taking a deep breath as I looked around, I was relieved to find myself in the cockpit of an airplane rather than the hallway of that hospital. Having to spend even one day in a place like that would give me the creeps.

The aircraft was picking up speed, and soon I felt the wheels pull away from the asphalt. Still a bit drowsy, I sensed the pilot had pulled way back on the stick, resulting in an unusually steep climb. Walt was impressed with the performance of his week-old aircraft, and he was particularly enjoying the speed and power of this takeoff.

But then, still at low altitude, there was a strange sound. Silence.

Suddenly, the engine was dead and we were losing all of our lift while plunging to the ground at 100 mph. We were experiencing an aerodynamic stall. Walt was frantically trying to restore power, but it was no use. There were no options. The engine was gone.

"That's it!" he cried. "We're going down!"

Because we'd been ascending at such a steep angle when the engine died, there was no gliding forward and no chance of even making a crash landing. As the nose of the aircraft pitched forward, we simply dropped to earth like a broken toy.

A huge tree loomed in front of the cockpit window and there was no time to brace myself. I didn't even have time to swallow before the Cherokee Six took full impact on its wing and midsection, hurtling me forward and slamming my face against the instrument panel. As the plane cartwheeled twice before skidding to a stop on its belly, the ruptured fuel tank spewed gasoline throughout the cockpit.

I lay there barely conscious for a few moments before the splattered fuel ignited into flames. As if in a dream, I felt bright, hot pieces of the sky falling on me. Although I waved my arms back and forth in a weak attempt to brush them away, the hot sky kept falling.

I didn't know which end was up. My mind was numb except for the stabbing impulse to escape. A voice in my head kept screaming, "Get out!" but my body couldn't obey. When I saw a ray of light pouring through the torn fuselage, I frantically pushed one leg through the hole to try to exit the plane. But my parachute harness was caught on something behind me, and no matter how hard I twisted or heaved, I was going nowhere.

Stuck like a fly in a web of burning metal, the adrenaline finally reached my gut and coaxed a sound from the only part of me that wasn't numb. If it hadn't been for my screams, I would have burned to death.

Until then, no one had realized the pilot and I were trapped in the cockpit. With only minor injuries, the other four skydivers had exited the plane immediately after it skidded to a stop. But on his way out, Dan stopped for a split-second to glance toward the cockpit. He saw Walt move but heard no cries for help, so he just assumed we were both okay and would be following him out of the plane.

Dan was just ten yards from the wreckage when he heard a loud whoosh! followed by the terrified scream of a man on fire. Going back into that plane was like running toward a bomb ticking off its last seconds. Still, he ran toward the sound of my voice.

The pilot's seat had crunched forward on impact, breaking Walt's legs and jamming them under the instrument panel. He moaned in pain while I screamed for help, each of us oblivious to the other's deadly predicament.

I don't remember Dan entering the cockpit. The right side of my body was on fire when I heard Dan's familiar voice say, "Help me, Mickey. Help me!" I twisted wildly with my last ounce of strength as two inhumanly strong arms heaved me out of the flaming undertow. With his bare hands, Dan slapped at the flames burning my head and neck while screaming over his shoulder, "I'll be back for you, Walt! Undo your seatbelt!"

But in the seconds it took to drag me clear of the wreckage, the cockpit exploded. When Dan let go of me to run back inside, he turned only to find it was too late. Walt's new airplane had become his funeral pyre.

I somehow managed to lunge fifteen feet further away before my fuel-drenched jumpsuit again ignited and I collapsed on the ground. Immediately Dan was at my side, rolling me back and forth until the last flame was quenched.

Now I lay, smoldering like a coal fallen from a furnace, next to the burning plane. "How bad?" I whispered. "How bad am I?" The words rasped sickly out of my throat as the right side of my face crisped.

"Can't tell, Mickey," Dan responded. "Don't talk. Just lie still."

I heard sirens and running footsteps and roaring like the sound of a bonfire after a homecoming game. The air was thick with the stench of gasoline and burning hair. Snakes of black smoke crawled in the sky above me, and faces, like human clouds, floated in and out of view.

Something was soothing the fear and numbing the pain. I was in the peace of perfect shock, and shock was a merciful hand lifting me out of my tormented body.

As white fingers slid an oxygen mask over my face, the blackened flesh just peeled off and slid onto the ground. Someone carried me through flashing red lights and thudding doors until I couldn't see the sky anymore.

As the whine of an ambulance pierced the air, pictures beat against my brain like birds escaping from a cage. My father's face as he caught the biggest fish of his life . . . my mother's small hands clutching rosary beads . . . Mickey Mantle slamming a ball out of the stadium and into the stars.

Then I saw a boy standing on a windy hill, and he was me. I heard a lyric repeating over and over, a mantra floating up through the dark waters of memory: Jimi Hendrix singing, *"Scuse me while I kiss the sky . . ."*

I remember thinking, *This must be the end.*

I had no way of knowing it was just the beginning.

Chapter Two

The Boy Who Loved the Wind

August 15, 1956

Standing fearlessly at the top of Midland Boulevard, roller skates strapped to my feet and tattered window shade in hand, I was ready for takeoff. In just seconds I'd be soaring high above the neighborhood. Looking down the hill, I was gathering the courage to launch out in this gale-force wind on my first flying adventure.

Ten . . . nine . . . eight . . . seven . . .

As I counted the seconds until takeoff, I half-hoped someone would step up to salute me on my first flight ever. But I was alone as I unfurled the shade and abandoned myself to the wind.

The clatter of skates on cement numbed my ears and made my teeth chatter as I rolled faster and faster down the hill. The billowing shade whipped and twisted wildly in the wind until, all of a sudden, I couldn't hear my skates anymore. I think I . . . maybe I . . . Yes! I was airborne! Come on, come on, higher, higher! Then—a flash of white light. Had I reached the clouds already?

The next thing I remember was being sprawled out on the concrete. As I blinked my eyes, I reached behind my head and felt a knot the size of a golf ball on my aching head.

Without a word I unstrapped my skates, swallowed hard, and trudged up the hill, like Orville Wright on a windless day. Just before reaching home, I plunged the wounded shade into a garbage can.

But I never trashed my dream of flying. I still believed Albert Einstein would come up with an anti-gravity formula, something like the little white pill that made smoke when I dropped it into my electric train.

After all, this was 1956.

As television fed me on its soft white bread of wonder, I anxiously awaited the coming of our brave new world. It was right around the corner, and I was definitely going to be part of it. Today the sidewalk, tomorrow the moon!

Already planning my next flight, I jerked open our kitchen door and grabbed a bottle of Coke. As I planted my-self in front of the television, the swamp-green screen glim-mered into a black-and-white image.

Suddenly there he was—the man of steel.

Able to leap tall buildings in a single bound. Faster than a speeding bullet, more powerful than a locomotive, he was the hero of every seven-year-old kid in America. As I watched him fly through the air, I couldn't help myself. Grabbing a towel and tying it around my neck, I leapt onto the armrest of our living room sofa and began diving repeatedly, imitating Superman.

"Mickey!"

Uh-oh. A lethal dose of krypton in the form of my mom!

"Get down from there! How many times have I told you not to stand on the furniture!"

My mother expertly removed my cape in one powerful jerk and gave me the ultimate warning.

"Not my clean towels—do you understand? Next time you use my clean towels, no more Superman!"

Walking into the kitchen, my mother added, "Your father has to go back to the shop this afternoon. He wants you to go with him."

It was a fate worse than death to be stuck with my dad on a summer afternoon. Most fathers would take their kids to a baseball game, or at least to the bowling alley. Not my dad. He made me sit there while he drank whiskey and played cards in some dingy bar.

I don't know why he always took me with him on these little outings. Maybe it was the only way he knew how to be a father. As I took my usual place on a vinyl barstool with a bag of potato chips and a shot glass full of cherries, I studied the man who lived in my house and called himself Mike Robinson.

My dad.

He was the youngest of six sons born to Michael and Eva Rochovitz. Born in St. Petersburg, Florida, in 1912, my father had changed his name from Rochovitz to Robinson in order to slide more tastefully into the racial stew that is called America.

He got his wish and slid right into the middle class. A machinist with four kids and a mortgage, Mike Robinson was the kindhearted guy next door who always worked too late and drank too much. I knew my dad was an intelligent man, even though he rarely spoke except to make snide remarks or crack a joke.

The real Mike Robinson was hidden away where no one could touch him, and not until I was a grown man did I uncover one of his best-kept secrets. At age 18, during the depression, my father had been sentenced to 11 years in prison for stealing $2.50 from a cash register. This was a crushing blow in his life. No matter how much he drank or how hard he worked, he was never able to overcome the shame of those depression years.

Like so many Americans in the '50s haunted by memories of war and loss, my father was a man on the run. Running from failure, he became a workaholic. Running from his heritage, *Michael Rochovitz* became "Mike Robinson." Running from his past, he became an alcoholic. Running from himself, he became a ghost.

And an embarrassment to me.

I wanted to be proud of my dad, but I hated his crude humor and rough manners. Watching him now in that dark bar smelling of cigarettes and bourbon, I vowed to be nothing like him.

Mike Robinson had the opposite of the Midas touch. Everything he touched turned to brass. Try as he might, he couldn't connect the dots on the picture of family life.

Although he and my mother shared a home, they might as well have occupied separate planets. She refused to live anywhere but Cleveland, but he never stopped talking about moving to Florida. She was a realist who went to mass. He was a dreamer who went fishing.

As the years went by, my mother's frustration had a volatile effect on my smoldering father. I was afraid to bring friends home because I never knew when sparks would fly.

I watched as my father walked an increasingly thin line between silence and rage. This became very clear to me the Christmas he gave me my dream-come-true, a Daisy BB gun. I couldn't believe my luck as I greedily unwrapped the slender package. My eyes must have been the size of baseballs as I held the coveted gift in my hand.

"Thanks, Dad!"

Reaching over to help me, he made sure I only attached the barrel that shot corks and not the one that shot BBs.

"When you're old enough to be responsible, I'll let you shoot BBs," said Dad in that I-know-what's-best-for-you tone of voice.

Yet, as the excitement of Christmas Day took its toll on a trigger-happy little kid, the inevitable happened. I accidentally shot a cork at my brother, who proceeded to howl like he'd been hit by a cannonball.

I knew my dad would be mad, but I didn't expect what happened next. I could actually feel the heat of his anger as he grabbed the gun out of my hand and bent it into a horseshoe over the back of the couch. I didn't say a word as I helplessly watched the best Christmas present I had ever gotten turned into a piece of junk.

Later he felt bad about losing his temper, but it was too late. Something in me broke right along with that gun. When my friends asked me what I got for Christmas, I skillfully pretended nothing had happened.

And pretty soon I became an expert at pretending. I turned a deaf ear to my parents' quarrels. I ignored the broken windows and broken promises. I simply closed the door on all the skeletons in the Robinson family closet and spent my time elsewhere.

Our house at 6708 Pleasant Valley Road became little more than a pit stop where I ate, slept and changed clothes. There was too much pain throbbing within those walls, so I unplugged myself from the family unit and turned toward the carefree world of friends and adventure.

I never tired of exploring the maple jungles of Ohio with my neighborhood pals. Together we found the tallest tree in the woods and built a tri-level fortress worthy of Robin Hood. In the topmost branches, we built a giant slingshot out of an old inner tube to protect ourselves from little sisters, inquisitive mothers and enemy tribes. When the alarm sounded, we'd head for the top of the tree to rain crab apples down on the intruders.

Life was simple. There was no obstacle I couldn't outclimb, outrun or outwit. The observation deck of our tree house was the highest place I'd ever been, and sitting up there gave me an intoxicating sense of freedom. The world looked completely different from 50 feet up, and I never wanted to come back down.

Mine was the generation of high hopes, while my parents had come from the generation of hard times. Although my mother and father were able to survive the harsh reality of the depression, something of life had been wrung out of them.

As a child of the '50s, I couldn't understand the hope-killing hardship they had endured. I just assumed they didn't know how to have fun. Although there weren't many "Kodak moments" for the Robinson family, there was one sacred pleasure my father and I were always able to share.

Every summer he'd drive us in our Buick up to a lake in Canada so we could attend what I called The First Church of the Holy Hook—his favorite church. Fishing was his religion of choice and the only part of Mike Robinson's world I was invited to enter.

Each morning we walked silently from our cabin through the cool, gray mist to the waiting water. There we performed the ancient ritual of loading poles and nets and boxes into an old bait-stained motorboat. As my father coaxed a sputter from the outboard, I pushed off from the dock into a world where we were no longer father and son.

On the lake, Dad wasn't old and I wasn't young. He wasn't distant and I wasn't ashamed. In that timeless place, we were just two fishermen waiting for silver creatures to float up through the dark water like manna from the deep.

We never talked. We didn't need to talk. It was enough being silent together. We sat on opposite ends of the boat from dawn until dusk, Dad feverishly absorbed in his quest for muskie while I waited for a lowly walleye or bass to strike my hook.

I think the closest Mike Robinson ever came to knowing peace was in that boat. It will always be my happiest memory of him. I don't know if he thought about God in those days. It wasn't something we talked about. I don't know if he even thought about eternity, but if he did, I'm sure his vision of heaven was a cold mountain lake brimming with fish.

On that lake, everything he touched turned to gold. He held the lodge record for muskie, and even had an article written about him in the *Cleveland Plain Dealer*. I was proud of my dad's success as a fisherman, even though he just couldn't make it as a family man. Maybe that was because he was a dreamer married to a realist . . . a realist whose vision of heaven had nothing to do with fish.

Chapter Three

The Bells of St. Michael's

My mother's vision of heaven was an altar where her four children stood before God in crisply ironed clothes and perfectly polished shoes. As a good Catholic, her job was to raise God-fearing children who would someday produce plenty of God-fearing grandchildren. And so my brother, two sisters and I each dutifully entered Catholic school at the tender age of six.

It was at St. Michael's in Independence, Ohio, that I met the god who walked softly and carried a big stick, but it was also there I met the god who inspired awe and wonder in my little-kid heart. Each Sunday morning, as I followed my mother up those ominous stone steps, I felt like an ant crawling into Yankee Stadium. Everything was huge and shiny and holy, but I would never go near the statue of Michael the archangel that stood outside the sanctuary. I was afraid if I so much as brushed his foot, the lifeless head might turn and stare into my murky little soul.

With Brylcreem'd hair and a white shirt buttoned almost to my eyeballs, I dipped my fingers in holy water while glancing painfully at my sister, Marilyn. Standing there, politely clutching a pink rosary in her white-gloved hand, she looked like a miniature adult. And that's what we were expected to be until mass was over. Until we descended those stone steps, there would be no whispering, no pinching, no giggling—only pious silence.

It's a little tough being pious when you're seven, but I didn't feel much like a kid as I gazed at the suffering Jesus on the Stations of the Cross. Those pictures made me feel like I was staring out the car window at the scene of an accident. And if I was ever tempted to utter a sound, my mother's withering glance instantly struck me speechless.

Mass was the only time I ever saw her sitting down, yet even in church she acted like a mother octopus. I thought she was the only woman on earth who could straighten my collar, pick lint off my sister's dress, make the sign of the cross and whack my brother on the head at the same time. My mother was fiercely determined to present her children without spot or wrinkle.

My mother wasn't overly soft or affectionate. She didn't hug me when I cried or lull me to sleep with bedtime stories, yet she held our family together with blood, sweat and tears. With little or no control over my father's downward spiral, she poured every bit of her amazing energy into keeping floors waxed and kids polished.

Secretly gazing at her in the half-light of the sanctuary, I could see the strain in her face. Though barely forty, my mother's countenance showed the weight of a miserable marriage. Yet Jean Gillombardo Robinson was the faithful daughter of Sicilian Catholics, and nothing could stop her from attending church. Although my father rarely joined us, except on Christmas and Easter, my mother never missed a Sunday mass.

As our little family sat quietly in the ruby and emerald light pouring down from the stained-glass windows, I felt a holy hush.

I had no trouble believing I was in God's house; I just had trouble picturing this person called God. I couldn't talk to Him except through a priest, and even then I couldn't tell him about baseball or Superman. The priest only wanted to talk about sin.

I couldn't understand God because he only spoke Latin. I couldn't tell him about my dream of flying because he wanted kids to sit still and keep quiet.

I couldn't touch Him, but for some strange reason He wanted me to eat His body and drink His blood. That was weird, but still I was intrigued in a seven-year-old kind of way.

So I spent my first year in catechism getting ready to meet God. It was kind of like Catholic boot camp, where the nuns led us through rigorous training for First Confession and Communion. It sounded simple enough: First we confessed our sins and then God came down to fill us with "sanctifying grace."

I didn't know what that was, but I was more than ready to be filled with it. I thought communion would be like the time Jimmy Knox and I pricked our fingers and let the blood run together, except, this time the sanctifying grace would run together with the wine to make me and God blood brothers.

When the big day finally arrived, my collar was buttoned so tightly my face looked like a cross between a tomato and the Goodyear blimp. But while marching single file down the church aisle with the other kids, I was seized with terror.

All of a sudden I knew I couldn't do this right. It wouldn't take me more than one little fight with my sister to blow my First Communion. I just knew I was going to sin again and lose my sanctifying grace.

I was headed straight for the curtain. What to do—what to do? Then I came upon a perfect plan. While walking back to my seat, I would make a beeline out of the church and head straight for Highway 21. There an oncoming car would squash me flat and beam me to heaven before I had a chance to lose my sanctifying grace.

I breathed a sigh of relief. It was the only way to make it into eternity without having to sit around wasting time in purgatory. I had a sneaking suspicion purgatory would be like the dentist's office—a weird white waiting room where you sweated bullets while listening to some kid scream for mercy down the hall. I had to make a run for it. Sanctifying grace or bust!

But when the time came for my heroic sacrifice, I chickened out. Walking dutifully back to the pew, I became just another church kid who knew what to do and when to do it. Yet, I still didn't know God. Not like I knew Mickey Mantle, a god of flesh and blood whose batting average was engraved forever in my heart.

I could soar in sports, but my Catholic career was a different story. I was continually tormented by my imagination. Whenever I had an impure thought, I tried to wash my mind out by closing my eyes and saying five Hail Mary's backwards. But my little formula wasn't working.

Each time I received the communion wafer dipped in wine, I sat in the pew with my fingers pressing hard against my eyeballs until colored lightning streaked the darkness. There were always blue dots mixed in with the colors, and these I associated with sin. The more blue dots, the more sin in my life.

There were way too many blue dots, probably because my flesh refused to shut up. It kept tapping me on the shoulder every Sunday morning and whispering, "I'm hungry."

Everyone was required to fast before communion, but as soon as mass ended I zoomed out of the church at breakneck speed and headed straight for Breck's Drug Store. There I jammed pretzel logs in my mouth while gulping a chocolate Coke, all the while feeling faintly guilty that my stomach wasn't more holy.

No matter how many prayers I prayed or confessions I made, I just couldn't skate around God the way I skated around everything else. My quick wit and confidence earned me the status of *cool* amongst the neighborhood kids, but these qualities didn't seem to impress God.

So I learned to fake it, and no one seemed to know the difference. Not until that day in the fourth grade when I had a close encounter with Father John.

Father John was a Polish priest who made Superman look like Howdy Doody. This man was 6'3" and 240 lbs., with a voice right out of the Old Testament. Not the kind of priest a kid wants to meet in a dark confessional.

When the little window slid open, my heart would melt like a popsicle. But in the next instant, I'd straighten up to meet the challenge. I could always fake my way through confession by reciting a laundry list of sins—though nothing more grisly than being mean to my little brother or talking back to my mom.

"Bless me, Father, for I have sinned."

"When was your last confession?"

"Last Wednesday, I think."

"What confession do you have to make, my son?"

"Um . . . this morning I spit in my brother's hot chocolate."

So far, so good. I sprinted through the basic stuff and then jumped right into the prayer of contrition. I was in the homestretch. I had recited this prayer so many times I could do it while standing on my head shuffling baseball cards.

"I . . ."

Uh oh. Mental jello. I went completely blank. How could I fake the prayer of contrition in front of a 240-pound priest? Seconds ticked by like hours. I slid both hands over my mouth, closed my eyes, and began swaying back and forth while mumbling the lyrics to my favorite song: *"We fired our guns and the British kept a-comin' . . . "*

Slowly this huge, shadowy figure on the other side of the confessional sat up in his chair and stopped me in mid-mumble.

"Young man!" he bellowed.

Oh, God, kill me now! I thought.

"Yes, Father?" I said.

"Do you know what you're praying?"

"Uh . . ."

"Do you realize you're talking to *God*?"

As he said the word *God*, I was certain that Charlton Heston was standing right outside the confessional, waiting to bludgeon me with a stone tablet.

"Without the prayer of contrition, there is no forgiveness for your sin. Do you understand that, young man?"

Oh boy, did I!

"And don't you ever forget that, as long as you live!"

I choked the words out, past the jagged lump in my throat.

"No, Father. I won't."

Somehow I made it through confession, but once outside I exploded in tears of embarrassment. From that day on, I did everything in my power to avoid Father John. Still, he made an indelible impression on me. I never again forgot the prayer of contrition.

A few months later, Sister Teresa talked to me about becoming an associate altar boy. Basking in glory for a moment, I made a quick re-entry into reality when she added, "Father John will be presiding over the mass."

I would have let out a bloodcurdling scream except for the fact that my body had become temporarily paralyzed. When the paralysis lifted, I ventured a squeak.

"Fa . . . Father John?"

"Yes, Mickey. You can pick up your cassock at the chapel after school."

Somehow I made it through the week and showed up at mass with my fingers clenched around the bell. My job was to ring it at appropriate moments when there was a long pause in the priest's prayer . . . a simple task for anyone who didn't have an ocean of adrenalin pouring through him.

I stood there calmly as Father John stepped into the pulpit. I waited there quietly as he started to speak in Latin. Then he breathed, and I rang that bell like I was Babe Ruth hitting a homer! When Father John glanced over at me with a strained expression, I assumed he just wanted me to ring harder.

So I did.

And every time he so much as blinked an eye, I rang that bell. It must have sounded like Santa Claus caught in the spin cycle of a Maytag washer, but I didn't care. With a terrified look on my face, I just kept ringing for dear life, and by the end of that mass, Father John looked a little scared himself.

And so I stumbled through my Catholic boyhood with a little grace and a lot of determination. Already skilled in the art of survival, I was the kid who could come out of any scrape with my hair combed and collar buttoned. Not until I was more than ten years old did I encounter anything I couldn't overcome with brains, luck or charm.

That year a friend sneaked one of his father's Playboy magazines out of the house and brought it to school. He was risking certain death by doing this, but the nuns never caught him. So when school was over, a small group of us headed straight for the far corner of a vacant lot.

Gathering into a tight, guilty little circle, we passed the magazine from sweaty palm to sweaty palm. When it came my turn, I waited to see if God would send a whirlwind to suck me swiftly into hell. I opened the magazine. Nothing happened. But as my eyes took their first glance at a naked woman, a clammy feeling clutched my neck.

The pictures made me excited and afraid, like sitting in a scary movie with one eye open and the other eye closed. I wanted to look, and I wanted to turn away.

Something strange settled in my soul that day. I felt like I'd touched hot tar, and it would never come off my hands. There was no hope for absolution, since I'd far rather be burned at the stake than tell a priest about that magazine.

There was no way out. I had to live with what I had done. Months went by and I never mentioned this to anyone—not until the day a young priest visited St. Michael's on his way to a mission post in South America.

He came out on the playground at recess to talk to us, and there was something different about him. He wasn't a voice behind a shadowy screen, but a real human being sitting next to me on the steps.

He didn't stare down at me, but looked directly into my eyes. He didn't call me *son.* He called me Mickey.

Pretty soon my friends and I began telling him things we'd never told another adult. Strangely enough, he didn't say anything. He just listened. Before I knew it, the cat was out of the bag.

"Father, I looked at a Playboy magazine."

I don't know what I expected next—chords crashing on a piano or trains going through a tunnel. Thunder at the very least. Instead I felt an incredibly gentle hand cover my head as the young priest made the sign of the cross, closed his eyes and spoke a prayer in Latin. I have no idea what he said, but in that moment something changed in me. I felt the shame melt away, as though the sun had come out on a winter day.

As I watched him pray for my friends, I remembered a picture of Jesus I'd seen once in a children's prayer book. At St. Michael's, the stained-glass saints had sad faces and empty eyes, but this picture showed Jesus in a field with kids all around him. He didn't look sad or pale. He just looked like a real guy who hung out with kids, kind of like that young priest.

I never forgot what happened that day. It was the first time I felt divine forgiveness shine through the haze of religion. Although it seemed like God still lived way out in space, I felt like He'd just paid a little visit to my playground.

Chapter Four

The Need for Speed

On a cold January day in 1961, I watched spellbound as our handsome new president took the oath of office. JFK had a perfect smile and lots of hair, which already put him way out in front of Eisenhower. But when I heard him say America would put a man on the moon before the end of the decade, he became my hero.

John Fitzgerald Kennedy was everything I wanted to be—an important guy who played football, looked like a movie star and talked about outer space. Since the day John Glenn first orbited the earth, I'd basked in the power and glory of the space program. I inhaled facts the way other kids ate peanuts. My bedroom was always plastered with magazine photos of astronauts, moon modules, and rocket launches.

If I'd been a kid in 1861, I would have packed my bags and headed West for adventure. But the West didn't sound so wild to me anymore. Space wasn't just the *final* frontier, it was the *only* frontier for a kid like me.

Even if I never became an astronaut, this was an awesome decade for becoming a teenager. The air hummed with possibility, but none of us ever imagined that the most memorable sounds of the '60s would include Walter Cronkite's special report.

One evening in 1962, while watching TV with my brother, the gray face of Walter Cronkite flashed onto the screen: "We interrupt this program to bring you a special report . . ."

I turned the TV up and called my dad. Special reports were few and far between, so when they appeared, America listened.

"Today President Kennedy demanded that Nikita Khrushchev, premier of the Soviet Union, remove all nuclear missiles from Cuba. Until this demand is met, the President has ordered a full naval blockade of that island."

All I needed to hear was the word *nuclear* to set my imagination soaring. Being a naturally inquisitive kid, I had poured over civil defense bulletins and studied everything I could about nuclear war. I crouched under my desk during all the "duck and cover" drills at school; I even stored cans in our basement so we could live on chicken noodle soup while civilization melted away.

Unlike most kids my age, I knew what the word *firestorm* meant. So the next day on the playground, I held a summit meeting with my three best friends. Together we called ourselves *The Four Aces*. Although it was pretty hard to look cool and ace-like in our weird green uniforms, we managed to pull it off. Maybe it was because the four of us were smart, athletic and irresistible to eighth grade girls.

We had each chosen an ace from a deck of cards, and then brazenly pasted it into the back of our school notebooks. I was the Ace of Diamonds, and for some reason this title made me feel responsible for the welfare of all thirteen-year-olds. I had to be a leader in times of crisis, and this was definitely one of those times. I knew if the Russians pushed a button, 300 million people would be dead in half an hour.

"What should we do, Mickey?" asked my friend Chuck, aka the Ace of Hearts. "You think we oughta put our bikes in the basement?"

I looked at him in disbelief. Obviously this kid had no idea what a 50-megaton blast followed by a 250-mph firewind would do to our nice little neighborhood. I was about to answer him with a snide remark when, all of a sudden, I had an idea.

"Hey, wouldn't it be cool if we made one last confession before it's too late?"

My friends looked like I'd just suggested we eat liver and brussels sprouts for lunch.

"Why would you wanna do that, Mickey?"

"I don't wanna die with unconfessed sins. Do you?"

"I guess not."

So with the zeal of Jesuits on their way to martyrdom, The Four Aces marched across the playground toward the rectory. Normally, I wouldn't be caught dead going there of my own free will. The rectory was a weird, off-limits kind of place—the habitation of dragons and black-robed priests. But today I felt brave. There's just something about nuclear war that makes a guy feel like getting right with God.

When I knocked on the big, wooden door, it slowly opened, like the door in *The Addams Family* show. The monsignor stood there calmly listening to our urgent request, and then without a word led us back toward the eerie confessional.

This time I wasn't kidding around. The nuns left no doubt in my mind that I could either face a priest or face eternal judgment. If Khrushchev pushed that button, I was only moments away from having to tell God my deepest, darkest secrets, so when it came my turn, I gladly spilled my guts to the priest.

When we stepped back outside, the world felt safer. It even smelled better. Although America was still on red alert, fear and worry had been lifted from me. Years later, I read that Kennedy had looked out from the White House balcony that same day and thought, *Tomorrow this will all be gone.* That's how close we were to a nuclear exchange.

But I was thirteen years old, and as soon as this crisis passed I turned my attention back to the dangerous business of growing up.

Only six months later, my Catholic school career came to an end. Standing by the mirror in my uniform that June day in 1963, I felt like a soldier being honorably discharged from duty. I couldn't wait to exchange the weird green tie and gray pants for civilian clothes. I'd served my time at St. Michael's and was now being promoted to the rank of teenager.

That fall I enrolled as a freshman at Independence High School and got my first job at Dairy Queen, making sundaes for 90 cents an hour. I ate all the mistakes and started saving up for the car of my dreams. Since my family's budget didn't allow for the fashion statement I wanted to make, I also began buying all my own clothes.

One of my first purchases was a fur parka that made me look like an Italian Eskimo. Definitely one-of-a-kind, it was made from some weird polyester that resembled the pelt of a mouse on chemotherapy. I was so proud of that coat, but my father just saw it as another excuse to needle me about my appearance. He never missed an opportunity to make fun of my desire to look good.

"Hey, pretty boy, you better look in the mirror. I think you've got a hair out of place," he'd say. "Don't forget to comb your jacket before you go out in public."

Outwardly I ignored him, but inwardly I counted the days. I couldn't wait to grow up and get out of that house.

I still went to mass, but it became just a duty I performed. Church had long ago lost its childhood aroma of awe and wonder. As far as I was concerned, going to mass was no different than putting a lightning rod on your roof. If you went to church, your chances of being clobbered by unforeseen disaster were significantly reduced.

But my nice little formula took a direct hit on November 22, 1963, with a report of the staccato pop of gunfire. I was taking some papers to the principal's office for my study hall teacher, but when I got there the secretary looked like she'd just seen a ghost.

"President Kennedy has been shot!" she cried.

I thought she was kidding. Things like this didn't happen in my version of America. I ran back to study hall and told my teacher, who promptly announced it to a bunch of bewildered ninth graders. Amid all the male wisecracks and female tears, I kept saying over and over, "How could this happen?"

He did everything right! Smart + Handsome + Rich + American + Catholic + President = Getting shot in the head at 44? This did not compute. Where was God?

The weirdness got weirder as television echoed the words *Dallas* and *Oswald* for what seemed like forever. I sat through mass that Sunday wondering why we even bothered to pray. If God couldn't protect Kennedy, maybe He couldn't protect anybody. An empty feeling crept over me every time some girl said, "Isn't Jackie brave?"

The shadow of national mourning drove me crazy. I had to get busy with something physical to block out my four-teen-year-old confusion, so during Christmas vacation I caught a ride to a ski area not far from Cleveland.

Although I'd always been a kamikaze sledder tearing down our neighborhood hills, growing up in Ohio had robbed me of my rightful place in the American legend. Surely if I'd grown up in Colorado, Jean-Claude Killy would have trembled at the name *Mickey Robinson*.

Walking into the ski shop in my rabbit fur parka and corduroy pants, I looked like Nanook of Cleveland. I plunked down my hard-earned money for skis, boots and poles, and then headed for the rope tow.

I was just about to climb on when I heard a distinctly female voice call my name. I turned and saw Val, an old classmate from St. Michael's. She came from a pretty wealthy family and was obviously no stranger to the sport.

She definitely outclassed me in her stretch pants and baby blue parka, but I was too excited to care about anything except getting to the top of that hill.

"Hey, Val! How ya doin'?"

"Is this your first time skiing?"

I guess the numbers painted on my boots must have given me away. "Yeah, I'm headed for the beginner's slope. Wanna join me?"

She smiled knowingly. "Not really. Why don't you come with me? I'll teach you everything you need to know."

It didn't take much to convince me, so we rode the T-bar up to the intermediate run and Val coaxed me down the first part of the slope. She skied slowly back and forth ahead of me while calling out instructions on how to traverse and form a snowplow.

"You're doing great, Mickey! You can make it by yourself from here on. I'll meet you at the bottom!"

As Val disappeared, I remember thinking how easy this was. I was just starting to get comfortable on the slope, when I came up over a hill and misplaced the ground. Those three minutes of downhill training Val had given me were no match for the banana-peel ride ahead of me on this, my first, mogul.

My poles made the sign of the cross as my butt skidded downhill at lightning speed. Unfortunately, that part of my anatomy was unable to form a snowplow, but within seconds my legs reunited with my torso as I slid to a stop.

Encrusted in ice and grinning from ear to ear, I couldn't wait to get up and try again. Again and again I headed down that mountain until I was transformed into that rarest of beings—a downhill racer from Cleveland.

Skiing wasn't just a cool thing I did on weekends—it was freedom for my soul. Instead of hanging out in the lodge schmoozing with girls or bragging about my exploits, I skied every available second. Although I didn't have much money, I purchased used equipment and bought cut-rate lift tickets from people leaving early. When the season finally ended March 15, I was still trying to squeeze one more run out of the muddy, melting slope.

It wasn't long before skiing replaced football as my favorite sport. Although I'd been a steady player at St. Michael's since the second grade, I'd just played my first football season at a "real" high school. The Catholic school always put out a lot of money for their sports programs, so I was used to playing in silk pants and fancy helmets.

But the ninth graders at Independence High School were considered no more than a farm team for junior varsity. We played on a practice field, and no one even came to our games. I felt like I'd just transferred from West Point into a mercenary army.

The glamour was gone. Yet when I rode the bus to my first game, that fall of ninth grade, I got that old adrenalin rush. As the coach made his way down the narrow aisle, I noticed he was looking right at me. Then he put his hand on my shoulder in a fatherly fashion, leaned down and said, "Robinson, we're short of players. I need you to play guard today."

I was stunned. I'd always been the running back at St. Michael's, and now he was changing my position one hour before the first game!

"But Coach, I never played that position! I've gotta be a back or a receiver . . . "

"We're not out here for personal glory, Robinson. We're out here to win. If you can't get with the program, then you shouldn't play on this team."

"Yes, Coach," I muttered, feeling like a man without a country.

I felt totally overlooked and out of place for the first time in my sporting life. I was switched to linebacker in the tenth grade, but changing positions didn't give me back the recognition I'd had in the eighth grade. Some of the childhood thrill was definitely gone, and to make it worse, the high school coaches even started to sound like my father.

"Blackie, fill in that hole!" yelled one coach while smacking me on the helmet. "This line is leakin' like a sieve!"

They called me Blackie because I had a dark complexion, but I didn't really care what they called me. I just wanted to belong. I wanted to be part of something. However, that desire came to an abrupt end the day I missed a practice play and the coach screamed, "Robinson! . . . OUT! . . . *Again*!"

That one remark burned me for years to come. I was giving football my best shot, but it didn't seem to matter. The coaches had their definite favorites, and I wasn't one of them. Activities had always been my means of soul expression, but now I was frustrated. Skiing was a definite high, but football wasn't doing it for me anymore. The slopes were only open a few months out of the year, so I had to supplement my thrill-seeking soul with a new fix.

Since I'd always excelled in solo sports, I decided to try gymnastics. I liked competing against myself. When it came time to break a record on push-ups or squat-thrusts, I always rose to the occasion.

There was no one in the gym during that first lunch hour when I threw a bunch of inner tubes on the floor, laid wrestling mats on top of them, and began to teach myself gymnastics. Day after day I worked out on the high bar, parallel bar and flying rings, doing inlocates, dislocates, cutaways and flips in the air.

I gave gymnastics my all, but I wasn't trying to earn a letter or win some championship. I was just doing it for the pure joy of movement. I assumed my body was immortal, so I naturally gravitated to the more dangerous moves and pushed myself to the limit.

Before long I became the first kid at Independence High School to do a giant swing on the high bar. But that still wasn't enough to satisfy me. No matter how fast or how perfectly I moved, it was never enough. I felt increasingly distracted, and could no longer find the release I craved. I was hungry—but for what?

Chapter Five

Somebody to Love

"Are you bored, Mr. Robinson?"

Mrs. Mackey stood next to me in the aisle, her body language communicating polite disdain. I looked up from my doodling and answered her honestly.

"Yes ma'am, I am."

"Well, I'm sorry to waste your precious time, Mickey. Would you please hand me that drawing you are holding? I'm going to get it analyzed, and maybe then we'll discover why you can't pay attention in class."

"If you find out," I said in all seriousness, "please let me know." My tenth-grade classmates snickered as Mrs. Mackey shot me the evil eye and walked back to her desk.

I wasn't a great student. Most of the teachers totally bored me, so I just drew pictures and got lousy grades. Yet for some reason, I did really well with demanding teachers and harder curriculum. Everything had to have the edge of competition for me to be even faintly interested. If it wasn't a challenge, it wasn't for me.

But being just an average student didn't interfere with my social life. I was an athlete, which naturally guaranteed me a space at the top of the teenage food chain. The winning combination was to be an athlete as well as being attractive—then you were really in. Crowded halls magically parted before males who could run fast, jump high, or catch a ball.

Luckily, I could do all three.

The gospel according to Mickey was pretty basic: I had to look good, stay excellent in sports and meet the right girl. So far I'd aced the first two requirements for a happy life, but the girl of my dreams was still a phantom.

It certainly wasn't for lack of opportunity. I did my share of flirting at dances in the gym, twisting my way across the polished floor with some perky little blonde in pink knee socks. And I was a regular at all the neighborhood parties where the ultimate goal was to get the lights turned off so we could slow dance to Johnny Mathis and make as much fumbling body contact as possible.

Yet there was no one special. Not until one winter night in 1965 when I arranged to meet a girl I knew at a party given by an old friend. Stepping down into the concrete basement filled with bubble hairdos and mile-high stacks of Motown albums, I was ready for a good time.

"Hey Chuck, you seen Sue?"

"She's over there. You going out with her now, Mickey?"

"Nah. No big deal. Just friends."

I spotted Sue and waved across the room. As we gravitated toward each other, I wondered why I wasn't more interested. She was cute. She looked good in a sweater. But there was no denying my lack of interest. I'd begun to wonder if I'd ever meet someone who could hold my attention.

Sue and I started doing our white middle-class best to dance like we were from Detroit. Everything was fine until she got a little too much soul and accidentally flung her hand into a metal pole. When a herd of girls whisked her upstairs for an ice pack, I dutifully followed them up to the kitchen. But when they started describing Paul McCartney's eyes, I had to leave.

Walking back downstairs, I stood on the steps for a minute just checking out the crowd. Suddenly everything froze as my eyes locked onto the face of a petite and pretty brunette. Although I'd known this girl since the second grade, I felt like I was seeing her for the first time.

"Some Enchanted Evening" should have been playing as we drifted toward each other through the sea of madras shirts and mohair sweaters. Her eyes shone like melted Hershey Kisses as I spoke to the girl of my dreams: "Hi, Julie. Long time no see."

She smiled. "I don't think I've talked to you since the eighth grade. You look good, Mickey."

"So do you."

When we danced, I knew she was the one I wanted to be with forever. I conveniently misplaced Sue of the swollen hand, and I didn't look at another girl the rest of the night. When it was time to go, I lightly touched the tip of Julie's nose with my finger and whispered, "I'll see you later."

That did it. We stood there burning our initials into each other's eyeballs while waiting for the room to stop spinning. When she finally drifted out the door, I stumbled to the back-yard for a cigarette with my old friend, Chuck. Grinning like a Cheshire cat while blowing smoke rings at the moon, I pulled out the 1923 Standing Liberty Quarter I'd carried in my pocket since I was seven years old.

"Here you go, Chuck," I said, casually flipping him my lucky piece. "You can have this. I don't need it anymore."

I didn't need luck now that I had Julie. She'd just filled in the last blank in my formula for happiness, and I proceeded to love her with all the passion of an ex-altar boy.

We became inseparable. Even though she was a junior and I a lowly sophomore, we leaned against lockers and stared deeply into each other's eyes for the next two years. After school we'd talk on the phone until we ran out of words, then just breathe meaningfully into the receiver. And even though Julie and I did our share of steaming up car windows at Garfield Park, we never slept together.

The sexual revolution hadn't quite made it to Cleveland, probably because the Midwest is last to join the party that moves from coast to coast. Whatever the reason, something always stopped us from going all the way.

Still, we had our struggles. One day she gave me back my class ring. Through tears, I frantically sliced the layers of yarn off the ring. My confidence disappeared as I imagined trying to survive without Julie. She mattered to me more than I was willing to admit.

Luckily, our split lasted only 24 hours. Although we made up the next day, I still felt dissatisfied. What I needed from Julie was guaranteed, unconditional, non-refundable love, and what I really wanted was for her to be my savior.

By this time, both my sisters had left home. They married right out of high school, probably in an effort to escape the sinking family ship. My brother and I still lived at home with an alcoholic father and a mother who was frantically trying to hold everything together. But her efforts were futile. She'd have been better off trying to straighten deck chairs on the Titanic. My family was going down fast in a sea of anger, alcohol and pain.

One night while on the phone with Julie, I heard the familiar sound of fighting coming from the kitchen. I hung up and walked directly into my father's line of fire. He looked at me coldly and said, "You still on the phone with that bit—?"

Those words shot through me like poison, and suddenly I was acting out the nightmares I'd had of my drunken father and me. Without thinking, I shoved him up against the wall.

My mother pleaded, "Mickey, don't! He is drunk! He doesn't know what he's saying. Leave him alone!"

But I could barely hear her for the sound of adrenalin rushing through my body. Memories clenched tightly in my fist, I punched him and broke the upper plate of his false teeth. Backing away from this pitiful drunk who was my father, I felt only disgust. As I banged the door open to storm out of the kitchen, I heard him mutter under his breath, "Thanks, son."

The defeat in his voice made my skin crawl. I couldn't stand the sight of him, so I moved to a friend's house for a couple of weeks. When I returned home, my father wouldn't even look me in the eye. We never spoke about what happened, but simply swept the incident under the rug along with all the other broken days.

I hated this part of my life. I hated the way it made me feel, but I couldn't fix it. I couldn't make it go away, so I cast a magic circle around myself. The agonizing frustration of home couldn't touch me once I was inside my magic circle. Friends and sports and Julie became the safety zones I ran for in order to keep my sanity.

By my junior year, I just had to play football. I needed to punch something, so I spent hours plowing into the seven-man blocking sled. Despite the sweltering summer heat, I found welcome relief.

Every time I rammed my body into an opponent, I was actually ramming my fist into whatever was destroying our family. Even the manager of the team noticed something had changed in me when he said, "Mickey Robinson is the hardest hitter we've got."

My name and number got announced over the loud-speaker pretty often that fall of 1966. I became adept at sacking the quarterback, and Independence High School had its best team record in 23 years. For the first time since those glory days at St. Michael's, it felt good to play football.

I didn't mind the grueling practice schedule, pushing my body past its limits, or getting up at sunrise day after day. When I stepped onto the playing field each Friday night, I forgot about the pain. When I faced my opponent, I felt powerful enough to tackle a planet and wrestle it to the ground. As soon as the ball was kicked, I was flowing with the one thing I craved above all else—adrenalin.

That fall of 1965, Julie was a senior and her name had been placed on the ballot for Homecoming Queen. She was more than a little miffed when she only made attendant, but I sent her a dozen red roses with a note saying, *You'll always be my special queen.*

On a magnificent October afternoon, I got to stand on the sidelines in my uniform and watch Julie pass by in a white

Mustang convertible. It was halftime and, as I took off my helmet, the roar of a thousand screaming kids greeted me.

The marching band screeched out "Hey Jude" as the Homecoming Queen and her attendants rolled slowly by. As Julie turned to flash me a smile, her tiara sparkled in the gold autumn sun. She was beautiful, and she was my girl. I felt proud.

That day seemed a good omen of our future together. The handsome football player would marry the pretty brunette, and we'd live prosperously ever after with our 2.2 athletically-inclined children. Like a game show contestant on a winning streak, I assumed any door we opened would yield happiness. Little did I know what lay ahead of us, not too far up the road.

Chapter Six

Runnin' on Empty

A lump formed in my throat as I read the inscription on Julie's senior picture that spring of 1966: *Dear Mickey... If it's meant to be, it'll be.*

Leaning up against her hall locker for the zillionth time, I asked, "Whaddya mean, 'If it's meant to be'?"

"I mean we'll see what happens when I get back from Europe," said Julie, matter-of-factly, as she neatly stacked books on the shelf.

"Europe?"

"Yeah, Janice and I are thinking about backpacking through Switzerland and France this summer. It's something we've always wanted to do."

"And what about me? What am I supposed to do while you're gone?"

"You'll be busy working and having fun. C'mon, Mickey, don't make such a big deal out of it!"

Everything seemed so easy for her. Why not? She was going to Europe and then on to college. I was looking forward to a sweltering summer selling popsicles at Isaly's Convenience Store. But there was nothing I could do about the injustice of the situation.

As it turned out, Julie's big travel plans never materialized. She ended up spending the summer at home, packing boxes and talking about college. Every once in awhile I got a weird feeling I was being shoved to the back of the bus, but I'd quickly shake it off. Although we were headed in different directions, Julie was still my soul mate. Of that I was certain.

When the fateful day finally arrived, I stood in her driveway, surrounded by piles of shoeboxes and suitcases. Leaving me with a kiss on the cheek and a promise to call soon, Julie jumped in the car and headed for southern Ohio to begin her freshman year at Miami University.

As she disappeared into the sunset, I braced myself for the final year of high school. I'd spent much of the last two years hanging out with Julie and her classmates, so now I was having to say goodbye to all my closest friends. Chuck was off to college, Mike was getting a job, Frank was getting married, and Dale was joining the army.

Lots of guys were headed to Southeast Asia, but the consequences of military service weren't real to me yet. Vietnam meant little more than green men in combat boots jumping out of helicopters on the six o'clock news. I couldn't imagine dying in a war that looked like a badly edited TV show.

But Vietnam was like a leaky faucet that never got fixed, and it just continued to drip until the pipes finally burst and flooded the basement of America. Then everything started floating to the top.

Universities turned into walled cities overnight as protests ricocheted from coast to coast. The word *revolution* became part of the daily vocabulary, and there was a thin column of smoke on the horizon from all the blazing flags, burning bras and smoldering draft cards. Times were changing everywhere.

Everywhere, that is, except in Independence, Ohio. Although we were beginning to hear wild rumors about jumping on a peace train, my high school was still chasing the caboose. The class of '67 wasn't allowed to wear jeans, tennis shoes or long hair, so most of us looked like fugitives from *Leave It To Beaver.*

This was the true weirdness of the '60s. An eighteen-year-old couldn't wear jeans to school in Ohio, but he could carry an M-16 to war in Vietnam. Something was definitely wrong with this picture, and as the war escalated and acid rock blasted into every brain, kids all around me began turning on and dropping out.

The music of the '60s wasn't just revolutionary; it was religious. Kids chanted lyrics the way priests chant prayer. My whole generation listened as songs poured into the air like invisible torpedoes and then exploded into bright fragments of social chaos.

Everyone had a personal anthem, and mine was by the group *Jefferson Airplane.* Something powerful grabbed me every time I heard Grace Slick sing, *"Don't you want somebody to love? Don't you need somebody to love? Wouldn't you love somebody to love? You better find somebody to love."*

Julie's absence had left a big hole in my life. Although I still skied and partied and played football, I was just killing time until graduation. I had no real career plans but I did have three solid goals for the future: stay out of the army, make a lot of money, and have an exciting life. I didn't care what I did as long as it had nothing to do with Vietnam, boredom or the middle class.

With Julie in college, I'd totally outgrown the senior scene. After football, there was nothing left to do except cruise until June and then grab my diploma. That's why I was kind of surprised the day my English teacher stopped me in the hall and said, "Mickey, can you come by the classroom later? I have something for you."

Carla Nesbitt was my toughest teacher, but she was also my favorite. All the kids liked this "with it" lady who related to them as human beings and not just like S.A.T. scores. Although I'd spent much of the year sitting in the back of her class making wisecracks, she liked me.

Maybe it was because of the theme paper I wrote on the subject, "What Would You Do If You Had 24 Hours Left To Live?" Everyone expected me to write something off-the-wall, but the day I read the paper aloud in class they were all shocked by my first sentence: "From the time a person is born, they begin to die."

Pausing a moment before reading on, I noticed guys fidgeting uncomfortably in their seats and a few girls rolling their eyes at each other. "Don't you think that sounds a bit negative, Mickey?" asked Carla gently.

"But it's true, right?" I remarked, and then went on reading. "If I had twenty-four hours to live, I'd want to spend it skiing down a mountain in Austria or running on a beach in Tahiti. But most of all, I'd want to make my mother smile."

I glanced over at Carla, who was looking at me rather intently. I think she saw something in me at that moment—something I didn't see in myself. From that day on, she became my friend as well as my teacher. Carla was one of the few adults I trusted, yet I really didn't know what to expect as I walked into her classroom that spring afternoon.

"You wanted to see me?"

Handing me a copy of *The Diary of Anne Frank*, Carla said, "I'm directing this play in April, Mickey, and I want you to try out for one of the lead roles."

This was the first time an adult had expressed interest in something other than my athletic ability. I was flattered, but I didn't let it show through my too-cool facade.

"Yeah, okay, I'll check it out."

"This is a very special play, Mickey," she said with uncommon seriousness. "Would you please read it over the weekend? I want you to try your hand at acting. I think you're a natural."

And she was right. When I read that play and met the character of Peter, I knew him. In an almost eerie way, I knew what he was thinking. Peter was a Jewish teenager trying to survive Nazi persecution in Holland, while I was a baby boomer trying to survive the '60s in America. We came from radically different worlds, yet our restlessness was the same.

Peter and I were both caged lions trying to break free of the family zoo. I knew I could tell his story better than anyone else, so I confidently headed to the school auditorium on the day of tryouts. But as I walked toward the stage, everything got quiet. I could feel all eyes on me.

"Hey, Mickey, what're you doing here?" asked Lisa, a girl who sat behind me in English.

"I'm trying out for the role of Peter."

"No kidding? Wow. You think you can make it through the first act without tackling Anne Frank?" Her message was loud and clear: jocks don't belong here. Rarely do teenage actors come from the ranks of the athletically-inclined.

Everyone was surprised when I got the part, and I even heard rumors that Carla had only picked me because I was good-looking. That remark stung me like a slap in the face and I became determined to prove them all wrong.

At first, all I cared about was making a big impression on my critics, but stepping into someone else's head was like entering a whole new world. Suddenly football seemed boring compared to what was happening on that stage.

In one of the scenes, I was supposed to run into my room and throw myself on the bed after being ridiculed by my father. As I did this, many people in the audience started to snicker, but something inside me immediately shouted, "No!"

I had to communicate the torment within this young man, so I jammed my face into the pillow and began to sob. At that moment, the audience fell silent and several people started to cry. *Now they get it,* I thought to myself. *Now they know what it's like to feel totally alone.*

A strange peace flooded me. For the first time in my life, I felt like I wasn't just screaming into an abyss. Somebody was actually listening. I'd made an emotional connection—but it felt much bigger than that. It felt like I'd just discovered fire.

As Carla Nesbitt witnessed my amazing transformation, she began urging me to seriously consider a career in acting. Although I was flattered by the idea, I just couldn't hold onto it. I had to live in the now, and right now my mind was consumed with Julie.

After Julie and I had an intense argument, I needed to talk to someone. Carla was the only adult willing to listen, but not even she understood the emotional importance of this relationship.

"I don't get it, Mickey. You're only seventeen! That's way too young to be getting serious. If I were you, I'd leave Ohio right after graduation and head for New York."

I was good looking and popular, so Carla naturally assumed I could confidently skate my way into a career. But she was wrong. I still had this gnawing insecurity that never went away, like a boogeyman that had stalked me since childhood.

It would disappear when I was doing sports or hanging out with friends, but then inevitably returned to whisper in my ear, "You're just fakin' it, Mickey, and pretty soon everybody's gonna know."

The only way I could keep it away was to stay busy and surround myself with people. I needed someone to hold back the loneliness, so I drank *activity* the way my father drank vodka.

"You don't understand, Carla. Julie is the most important thing in my life. I'm not going anywhere without her."

She looked at me the way most adults look at love-struck teenagers—like they've forgotten what it's like to feel passionate about anything.

"Okay, but I think you're wasting a good opportunity. Take my word for it, Mickey. The older you get, the harder it gets."

She was trying to steer me clear of an emotional pothole, but I didn't heed the warning. And after the play was over, Carla stopped talking about my acting career. She politely let go of my destiny, and high school settled once more into a boring routine.

I somehow made it through until June, but just a few days before graduation, my guidance counselor called me in for a final interview.

"What are your plans, Mickey?"

"I don't know. Maybe I'll apply for my old job at Otis Elevator. I worked there last summer and made a lot of money. It'll be okay," I explained, giving Mrs. Patterson a winning smile. "At least until something better comes along."

"Aren't you at all concerned about the draft?"

"No. I'm not going to Vietnam. I'll figure something out."

"Well, I wish you luck," she said, giving me that "poor dumb kid" look. "I hope everything works out for you, Mickey, but sometimes . . ."

"I appreciate your concern," I said, interrupting her as I stood to my feet. I could tell she was revving up for a lecture on responsibility, so I just politely excused myself and walked out of the office. I wasn't worried about my future. I knew something would come along.

And I was right.

Chapter Seven

Wall Street Wonder Boy

Just one day before graduation, I sat down to check the classifieds and I spotted a job opening at a brokerage firm in Cleveland. Sitting there with newspaper in hand, I fantasized about little men in white shirts shouting and waving papers as buzzers and horns blared in the distance. It was a football scrimmage without helmets—the perfect job for someone like me.

I immediately put on my checkered sport coat and drove downtown to let them know it was me they were looking for. Walking confidently into that personnel office, I felt like Zorro on his way to fencing lessons.

After filling out the application and handing it back to the secretary, I ventured to ask, "Have many other people applied for this position?"

She smiled. "About 300 so far."

I didn't feel like Zorro anymore, and walked out of that office with few expectations. I was only seventeen and had no experience, so I figured my chances were almost nil. But surprisingly, they called me back for an interview.

As I sat across the desk from the company's personnel director, I tried to look like I knew what I was doing.

"So, Mickey, tell me why you want this job."

"Well, sir, what you need to know about me is that I'm always where the action is. I'm up for any challenge, and I don't care how long the hours are."

Even though young and inexperienced, I seemed confident. And I was definitely good looking. If looks could get me into that brokerage firm, I knew I could dazzle them with charm and energy. After the interview, the personnel director walked me to the door and then abruptly turned to shake my hand.

"Congratulations, Mickey. You start Monday."

I wanted to pass out cigars, but I swallowed my enthusiasm and calmly answered, "Thank you." All the way home I played mental Monopoly, imagining myself sliding dozens of red hotels onto Boardwalk with my fist full of $500 bills.

When I finally jumped out of the car and burst through my mother's front door, I couldn't hold it in any longer. Intoxicated with my own success, I shouted, "I'm in! I'm gonna be a Wall Street wonder boy!"

The market was at flood stage as I took my first steps into the river of glorious greed. They sat me down at a table with five other people and gave me two phones, a headset, a yellow legal pad and very simple instructions: MAKE MONEY.

My job was to buy and sell over-the-counter stock, and that's basically all I did eight hours a day. It was a rare moment when I wasn't on both phones taking orders and translating them into sales as fast as I could. There was so much frantic energy in that office, I had to flip paper clips and scribble madly just to keep from going into orbit.

I watched fortunes being won and lost on a daily basis, but it wasn't really the money that turned me on. It was the speed. We were riding a roller coaster that either climbed to the stars or derailed on the curve. I surrounded myself with hard-driving people who wanted more, and it felt glamorous.

My aggressive young boss sat only a few feet from me, swigging from a bottle of Maalox, smoking a cigarette and talking on two phones, all at the same time. This guy was a millionaire at age 29, so I decided to watch every move he made.

Primed and ready for war first thing every morning, he approached the starting gate by saying, "Okay, you guys, we're gonna get 'em today. Put on your game faces and let's go!"

There was no time to get warmed up. We had to be hot when the bell rang and stay hot on adrenalin, donuts, coffee and profit. Sitting there, surrounded by ringing phones and sweating co-workers, I felt like a dispatcher on D-day. My job was one long jolt from start to finish.

Everything amazed me. This was the first time I'd ever seen anything digital, and right in the middle of our office sat a Xerox machine as big as a car. Everything looked state-of-the-art, or at least I thought so, until the day a computer guy showed up to plug us into the brave new world.

As he installed what came to be known as *the system,* I watched spellbound. Computer technology hadn't yet made it to the suburbs of Cleveland, so this looked to me like something out of a James Bond movie. The installer didn't say much, but on his way out he left us with a parting word of wisdom: "People can fail, but the system can't fail."

No one spoke, but we all looked at each other as if we'd just heard from God. I was still pondering the enormity of his parting remark when the firm's vice president called me into his office.

"Mickey, I've got some cash, checks and negotiable stocks to go to National City Bank right away. Can you take them for me?"

"Sure, no problem." The bank was only a few blocks away, and since it was a cool September day, I decided to walk. As I grabbed the briefcase and started out the door, he laughed and said, ""Hey, be careful! You've got half a million dollars in there!"

Our office was right in the center of downtown Cleveland, so the sidewalks were packed with people. As I threaded my way through the crowd, I felt more and more like a big shot. It's amazing what carrying half a million dollars will do for your ego.

Nobody has any idea what I've got in here, I thought to myself as I tightened my grip and looked straight ahead.

When I walked into the bank, they politely escorted me to an office on the second floor that smelled of leather and money. As I sat there waiting for some VIP to show up, I felt genuinely important for the first time in my life. They were grooming me to be somebody.

I even started carpooling for success. Every day at five o'clock I'd catch a ride home with Brian, one of our accountants. I'd climb into his Valiant, turn on the radio and try to breathe, in spite of the suffocating haze of English Leather and cigarette smoke. As we glided through the streets of Cleveland, he grilled me with a white-collar version of *Twenty Questions.*

"So, Mickey, how much money do you want to make?"

I felt like saying, "That's kind of a stupid question, isn't it?" But I restrained myself. Squinting at him out of the corner of my eye, I noticed he looked a little like Scrooge McDuck counting his stacks of money. This guy was absolutely serious, so I played along.

"Uh . . . as much as I can!"

"Are you planning a long-term career in the market?"

"Yeah, I like the speed. I think I can go places as a trader."

"Some of us are taking evening classes. Are you interested in getting more education?"

Now I wanted to cuff the guy on the head and say, "Mellow out, will ya?" But Brian was one of those guys whose eye was on the prize. I, on the other hand, just couldn't get that excited about climbing the corporate ladder. Although I wanted to make money, I knew my soul would shrivel up and die if I tried living off a list of things to do.

But I sure was enjoying the prestige of my job. All of a sudden, powerful businessmen in three-piece suits were taking me to lunch at the Pewter Mug. My previous experience of sit-down dining was limited to Sunday lunch with my family at a little Italian restaurant, so this was a whole new ballgame.

During my first lunch with the boys, I tried to look sophisticated while everyone ordered stuff I'd never heard of before. I decided on the chef salad because it sounded like something a stockbroker would eat.

"What would you like for lunch, sir?" said this amazingly soft voice.

When I looked up from the menu, there was this awesome waitress in a leather miniskirt standing right in front of me. She smiled. I smiled. We both smiled, and I forgot about lunch.

"She's waiting for your order, Mickey," said one of the guys impatiently.

"Oh yeah, I'll have a chef salad!"

"And what would you like to drink with that, sir?"

Luckily I'd just seen the movie *Goldfinger,* so I still remembered James Bond's drink of choice. But there was one little problem: I was eighteen, and the drinking age in Ohio was twenty-one. Yet I was sure everyone thought I was older. No eighteen-year-old would be hanging out with such important business types.

It was worth a try.

"A martini, please." I had no idea what I was ordering, but it had to be incredible because James Bond drank it.

"Vodka or gin?"

"Pardon me?"

She smiled knowingly. "Would you like that martini made with vodka or gin?"

My dad always drank vodka, so I ordered gin. When the waitress placed a very cool-looking glass in front of me a few moments later, I instinctively grabbed it and gulped. Trying to remain calm, I fought the immediate impulse to wash my mouth out with beer. Instead, I inhaled a forkful of salad while mentally placing martinis on my list of untouchable substances. They ranked right up there with liver.

But martinis and power lunches were only part of my initiation into the mysteries of the city. Culture shock really hit when I encountered the fast-moving females known as *city girls.* There were a lot of them in my office, and they were fast—a little too fast for this Catholic kid from the suburbs.

One balmy summer night, six of them decided to escort me to a Johnny Mathis concert at the Music Carnival. We all sat around a table in a huge circus tent with the sides rolled up, while I turned up the charm in order to impress my one-night harem.

When they dimmed the lights, a silver ball twirled overhead and tiny stars began to dance on the ceiling. As Johnny sang his velvet version of "Eleanor Rigby," one lovely young lady reached under the table and slid her hand gently into mine. It felt like high school.

We all went to her house for a nightcap afterward, but for some reason, everyone took off and left me sitting all alone. The next thing I knew, my hostess strolled out of the bedroom in her robe, sat down beside me, pressed a drink into my hand and invited me to stay awhile.

"Uh, no thanks. It's really late, and I've gotta get home." I'd had a fun evening flirting with the girls, but I had no intention of spending the night. Maybe it was because I had to work early the next morning, or maybe it was just because of Julie.

I'd really been missing her, so I planned a trip down to Miami University for the big homecoming game. She made plans for me to stay at a fraternity house, and I couldn't wait to meet all her friends and impress them with my corporate status.

"Hey, Nathan, this is Mickey," announced Julie as we walked up to one of the frat house inmates. "You know, the guy I told you about? The one who works for a stockbroker in Cleveland?"

From the guy's deadpan expression, Julie might as well have said, "He picks up horse manure after parades." He didn't even extend his hand, but sized me up with one glance before turning his attention back to Julie. While they talked, I looked down at my legs to make sure I hadn't become invisible.

I got this same cool response from most of her classmates. It didn't take long for me to realize collegiate-types are only impressed by other collegiate-types. My position in the stock market was of little or no interest, probably because it didn't fit in with their unwritten statement of purpose: *I study, therefore I am.* Unfortunately, that left me out. I worked, therefore I wasn't.

But I didn't let it bother me. After all, there was still Julie and the big game. That Saturday morning we shoved our way into the packed bleachers, hugging, laughing and getting high off the crisp autumn air. Trumpets blared, drums pounded, and cheerleaders flipped as Julie cuddled next to me to keep warm. This was one of those days when it felt good to be alive.

Miami University was playing Bowling Green, and whenever Miami scored, I screamed my head off. This wasn't my school, but it was Julie's, and that was reason enough to jump up and down and shake my fist at the opposing team. I kept taking swigs from a bottle of Stroh's beer hidden inside my coat, so by halftime my bladder was screaming for mercy. But when I stood up to walk to the bathroom, I heard a droning noise overhead.

I thought maybe it was just a beer buzz, but then I looked up and spotted a plane circling the stadium at an altitude of about 5,500 feet. My wandering attention immediately focused when the side of the aircraft opened and miniature men began falling out in perfect synchronization.

I could hear a faint *whoosh* as members of the U.S. Army Parachute Team tore through the atmosphere. Then, as puffs of black and gold burst above them in the sky, they drifted to earth like seeds in a summer breeze. When one of the skydivers floated directly over where I was sitting, my eyes followed him down to a perfect precision landing.

At that second I made a silent vow.

I'd read somewhere: *A man who makes a vow makes an appointment with himself at some distant time or place.* On that day, I made an appointment to meet myself in the sky.

When the exhibition was over and the band started to play, I whispered out loud, "I'm gonna do that."

"What'd you say, Mickey?" asked a familiar female voice. Although Julie had been sitting next to me the whole time, I'd forgotten all about her. I was totally focused on the sight of those black and gold parachutes.

"Uhhh, hello, earth to Mickey!" laughed Julie as she rapped me on the head with her knuckle.

I smiled at her numbly, still lost in thought. Something that would change my life forever had just passed before my eyes, but I couldn't talk about it. Sacred things disappear when you try to explain them, so I just tucked it away and wandered off to the bathroom.

Chapter Eight

Bad Company

An old friend was waiting for me when I arrived at work that Monday morning. I'd known Danny since the first grade at St. Michael's, where he'd single-handedly convinced several nuns to reconsider their vocation. Danny was the kind of kid that adults warn you about, like that little devil that stands on your shoulder and tells you it's okay to put the cat in the dryer.

"How come you're showing up here on a work day, Danny?" I asked sarcastically. "Did you accidentally set fire to your boss over at Merrill Lynch?"

"Nah—I quit!" Danny said flippantly. "I'm not gonna spend the rest of my life in Cleveland. How about coming with me to Florida, Mickey?"

The truth was he'd just gotten fired, but I decided to listen to his little spiel anyway. And the longer I listened, the brighter the sun seemed to shine. There was just something fatally charming about Danny, and my conscience keeled over dead every time he opened his mouth.

"What do you have here in Ohio, Mickey? Sub-zero temperatures and a car that won't start? We could be lying on a beach right now! Wake up and smell the coffee, Robinson."

"Yeah, maybe. But I'd have to give two weeks' notice."

"No way. You don't owe these people anything. They can replace you in a heartbeat. Just go home and get packed—we're going to Florida, buddy!"

Danny insisted we leave right away, so I didn't call the office the next morning to tell them I wasn't coming in. I never even told them I was quitting. Instead I just jumped into Danny's little sports car and headed south in a blaze of irresponsibility. The one thing I did do was make Danny stop for a few hours in Miami, Ohio, so I could let Julie know about our big plans.

I thought she might be mad at me, but for some reason she seemed unusually attentive.

"What're you planning to do down there, Mickey?"

"I don't know. Get a job. Go to the beach. Maybe I'll check in with a broker in Ft. Lauderdale. I can get a job anywhere!"

"Are you planning to date other girls?" she asked with a blank look on her face.

It was kind of nice being on the high end of the relationship teeter-totter. Usually I was the insecure one, but for one brief moment the tables were turned.

"There's never gonna be anybody but you, Julie. Don't you know that by now?" I assured her, holding her in my arms. "I'll be calling you every week, just like always."

When Danny and I finally drove into Ft. Lauderdale, the streets were lined with red convertibles and bronze flesh. Blonde hair sparkled in the sun and the salt air smelled of tanning oil and heat. It was a far cry from the gray streets of Cleveland filled with dark suits and tired faces.

We moved into a furnished apartment near Sunrise Boulevard, but the only thing we had was our clothes. At first, Ft. Lauderdale seemed like an endless Friday night, but after just a few days I started feeling homesick for a Monday morning. Sunrise and sunset had become one big blur, and I didn't like living in a town where youth was the only serious occupation.

Danny kept talking about looking up a musician he'd met once in Cleveland, so we headed over to the guy's apartment and found him sitting in front of three television sets, watching basketball.

"You guys wanna come with me to the club?" he asked while shoving pizza boxes off the coffee table and kicking beer cans under the couch. "Don't you think Lauderdale is a great town? I love this town."

When we got to his club and sat down at the bar, he immediately tried using Danny and me to hustle women.

"Hey, Mickey, see that good-looking girl over there? Why don't you ask her to come over and have a drink with us?"

I looked at Danny, who was sitting there with this stupid grin on his face. He didn't seem to mind Mr. Schmooze, but the guy made me nauseous. Ft. Lauderdale was beginning to feel like a watering hole for shallow people with raging hormones.

I'd made one weak attempt to apply for work at a brokerage firm, but my heart wasn't in it. I didn't dare tell them about Cleveland. There was no way I could ask for references from a job I'd just run out on, so I started stacking shelves in a grocery store just to meet expenses.

After spending one afternoon designing toilet paper displays, I was desperate. I'd only been in Florida one week, but already I knew I'd made the biggest mistake of my life.

Danny was content to sleep all day and party all night, but I couldn't live like that. I felt totally ashamed, and this time there was no understanding priest ready to offer me absolution. Flat broke and more than a little embarrassed, I anxiously looked for a way out.

My answer came unexpectedly in the form of Rob, an old friend of Danny's who'd flown down for a week of serious hedonism. Rob had just gotten out of the army and was exploding with hype. The guy never stopped talking, and his favorite subject was himself: how smart he was, how exciting he was, and how much money he could make. I tried my best to steer clear of him until one night when he made me an offer I couldn't refuse.

"Hey, Mickey, there's this snowbird who's hired me to drive his Cadillac back to Toronto. You want to come along for the ride? I'll split expense money with you."

This was it. The moment I'd been waiting for—escape from Sunrise Boulevard.

"You mean it?" I exclaimed. "When do we leave?"

I could feel Danny glaring at me. I hadn't told him how much I hated Florida. I knew he'd never understand why I wanted to leave his fantasy world of wine, women and song.

"What's the matter with you, Mickey? We just got here!" Danny retorted. "You can't tell me you'd rather be in Cleveland?"

"Yeah, Danny," I said as I turned and looked him straight in the eye. "That's what I'm telling you. This is your scene, not mine. No hard feelings, okay? I just gotta go."

He turned and walked out of the room without saying a word. In fact, he stopped talking to me altogether. But this time I didn't care. I'd been in Florida six weeks, and that was five weeks too long, as far as I was concerned.

It felt good to break free of Danny's influence and do what I knew was right. I was pretty proud of myself, at least until I jumped into the Cadillac the next morning and realized I was taking a road trip with a maniac.

Danny may have been a bad influence, but Rob was truly crazy. He kept insisting on telling me everything I never wanted to know about him, like how he'd been kicked out of school nine times before joining the army. He especially enjoyed describing, in vivid detail, all his misadventures among the prostitutes of Barcelona and Amsterdam.

I kept one ear tuned to Rob's colorful confessions while the other ear listened anxiously for the sound of a police siren. I was convinced we were setting an all-time speed record for the eastern seaboard.

Rob insisted on a cruising speed of 90 miles per hour. Once in awhile he would hit the brakes and swerve into a station so we could get gas and make a run for the bathroom, but we never stopped to sleep.

The trip only took 22 hours, but they were the longest 22 hours of my life. We lived on coffee, Cokes and candy bars until midway through the trip, when Rob's stomach forced him to pull over at a roadside cafe. He quickly wolfed down his food, jumped up from the table and said, "Let's go!" while heading straight for the door.

"What about the check?" I whispered in disbelief.

"You want to pay? Go right ahead—I'm leaving."

I didn't have any money on me, so I guiltily scurried after him, like Igor following Dr. Frankenstein out of the graveyard.

In the morning, while driving through North Carolina, we came across a flock of chickens making their way across a lonely stretch of road. I held my breath as Rob slammed his foot down on the accelerator and cackled, "Here we go!" When I sheepishly opened one eye to peek out the back window, all I could see was a grisly cloud of chicken parts, feathers and dust. In addition to my other failings, I was now an accomplice to murder.

Rob had the personality of a train wreck, but I was a captive audience. I already felt like a loser, so I was more than open to any suggestions he had on how to put my life back together.

"Gas grills. That's the way to go, Mickey. Install gas grills. There's this company that pays salary plus commission. The faster you work, the more money you make. Sound good?" he asked, grinning at me like some weird army recruiter.

Miraculously, I survived the trip. After dropping the car off in Toronto, I took my share of the expense money and immediately jumped on a commuter flight to Cleveland. It was mid-March and, as luck would have it, we flew right into a blinding snowstorm.

There was a foot of snow on the ground as the aircraft slid sideways down the runway and then stopped just short of crashing into the terminal. It seemed like an appropriate end to my desperate little adventure. The temperature was eight degrees below zero as I disembarked, looking like some kind of idiot in my aloha shirt.

I felt guilty and ashamed, like an alcoholic returning home after a drunken binge. I arrived with no money, no job and no prospects, but thankfully I still had somewhere to go.

Walking into my parents' house, I breathed my first sigh of relief in several weeks. I was so glad to be home that I hardly even flinched when my brother told me how bad things had been.

"Dad's drinking got real bad, Mickey. He's started going to A.A. meetings, and Mom goes with him."

"You think it's helping?"

"I don't know. I guess it's too soon to tell. He's trying, though."

When my parents came home, they didn't ask much about Florida and I didn't volunteer any details. They were preoccupied with their own troubles. My mother was desperately trying to help my dad stay sober, but it was a losing battle.

Six weeks later, he went back to drinking straight vodka first thing in the morning. It wasn't long before my mother's patient endurance came to an end. After twenty-five long years, she finally asked my father for a divorce. As he made a shame-filled exit from our broken home, Mom took a full-time job as a waitress just to survive.

I chose to stay with my brother and my mother, and that meant I had to find work immediately. I was too embarrassed to apply for anything in the stock market, but I was desperate so I took Rob's advice and started installing gas grills.

Thankfully, the company didn't ask for references. It was the kind of place where nobody cared whether you were a college graduate or a serial killer. If you could handle a screwdriver, you were in.

After basking in the glow of the stock market, this was a very humbling experience. There was no charisma here. No prestige. No power lunches. Just money. I felt like I'd blown my big chance in the business world, and I was now holding a card that said: Do Not Pass Go—Do Not Collect $200. But, as always, I was sure something better would come along sooner or later.

Since there wasn't much excitement in my life at this point, I got together with some former high school friends and we smoked hash. We thought the fastest way to alter our consciousness would be to ingest drugs in a psychedelic setting, but Cleveland was a far cry from San Francisco. If we were going to plug into something cosmic, we had to take matters into our own hands.

So we improvised. We removed the multicolored rotating lights and motor from an old aluminum Christmas tree. We covered it all with a blanket, and then we stuck it in the rafters of my parents' basement. It diffused the light in eerie patterns across the ceiling, giving the room a psychedelic effect. Next we lit candles, burned incense, and tried hard to enter a new dimension. I have to admit our efforts were greatly enhanced by drinking Stroh's beer and listening to Jimi Hendrix cranked up really loud.

About that same time, my sister's friend got us tickets for a Hendrix concert—in the second row, no less! This was sure to be an historic event, so I had to dress appropriately. But by that time, my wardrobe had definitely taken on the look of a gas grill installer.

I had nothing even slightly cosmic in my closet, so I decided to wear an old white pajama top covered with maroon blobs. And to this, I added a necklace of wooden bear claws borrowed from my sister. Walking into the auditorium that night, I looked like Ozzie Nelson after a grizzly attack.

The people around me dressed like real hippies, but I looked like a kid ready to go trick-or-treating. I didn't even have any dope on me. Elbows and love beads kept jabbing me in the back as the crowd pushed hard to get through. The air was so thick with patchouli, marijuana and sweat, I could hardly breathe. All the hard-core music people had turned out to see Hendrix. Tonight was *the* event of 1968 in Cleveland, Ohio.

The stage was stacked with six Marshall amplifiers and twelve cabinets as this 90-pound guy wearing a black hat, skintight jeans and a leather vest slithered toward the microphone. His face was like a long, thin mask, and he moved like he was made of rubber bands instead of bones.

When he picked up the guitar and started to play, something huge began swallowing him chord by chord. A sound like trains derailing or stars colliding exploded into the arena, and as I watched him, I had this weird feeling he was no longer with us. Jimi had disappeared into a black hole and was now beckoning us to follow him into this wonderland. His music wasn't shattering glass. It was shattering dimensions.

The crowd mindlessly mouthed words as Jimi snapped and slid across the stage like a live wire. As I looked around, I saw face after face aglow with desire. I knew they would gladly hurl themselves into an abyss just to hear what he was hearing. They would sell their souls to feel what he was feeling. *Life Magazine* had just labeled him a "demigod," and tonight he was surrounded by his disciples.

I could see how he was coming on to the crowd. I happened to glance offstage, and there behind the curtain stood a group of adoring young women obviously waiting to be with him. The intensity grew and grew until he finally ended with a mind-bending version of "Wild Thing," smashing his guitar and falling to his knees mumbling, "Stoned . . . stoned."

Only then did I understand why he had to destroy his guitar. It was the only way he could stop the music. As Jimi knelt there limp and lifeless, the crowd went insane and stormed the stage. Being in the second row, I had no choice but to move forward or be squashed by an ocean of bodies. All around me people were chanting "Jimi! Jimi!" while desperately trying to climb onstage, as if touching his boot would be like touching the Holy Grail. I couldn't relate to them, but I felt jealous of their passion. I wished I could want something that bad, or believe in someone that much.

As we drove home, everyone was unusually quiet. The mood and conversation in the car that night bordered on the weirdly religious.

"Jimi was electric, man."

"His music took me someplace—I saw stuff I've never seen before."

"I was traveling with Hendrix on the astral plane."

"What a bummer that people rushed the stage at the end. Poor Jimi . . . "

That was the final straw. I looked at my friend and said, "Whaddya mean, 'Poor Jimi?' He was beggin' for it! You don't think he wants all that attention?"

The next day I read in the paper that Jimi Hendrix picked out a new Corvette while he was in town, paid cash for it and then drove off into the sunset.

That concert only added to the deep conflict in my soul. I was confused by all the events of the past few months— quitting my job, living in Florida, watching my parents split up, smoking dope and hanging out with people intent on worshipping a guitar player.

All the lyrics talked about peace and freedom, but I didn't feel peaceful. And I sure wasn't free. People around me kept pointing to his music and telling me it was truth, but I wasn't impressed. I was still searching, but I knew one thing for sure—if there was someone worth worshipping, I wouldn't find him acting out such perversion.

Chapter Nine

Passing Go

One spring day in 1968, I walked through the front door after work to hear my brother yelling, "Somebody call a plumber! The toilet's about to blow!"

I quickly grabbed a phone book and began flipping through the yellow pages. I had just reached the *Ps* when suddenly I saw it. There in bold, black letters were the words:

Medina Parachuting Club

No experience necessary.

Call for information.

I immediately forgot about the plumber and dialed the number.

"Medina Parachuting Club."

"I'm interested in taking some classes in skydiving. When could I start? . . . Hello?"

There was a weird silence on the other end. I thought we'd been cut off, but then the voice answered, "I'm sorry, but we're not taking new students right now. Would you be interested in flying lessons? We're offering a special rate."

Only later did I discover that the club had shut down. Most of their members had been killed in a skydiving tragedy over Lake Erie the previous year. On August 27, 1967, eighteen skydivers exited the plane after receiving radio clearance to jump, but the ground station mistakenly had another aircraft in sight. The skydivers weren't over the target area, but were actually flying over Lake Erie. Due to the dense cloud cover, no one realized the error until it was too late. Eighteen skydivers went into the lake that day, but only two came out. The other sixteen drowned.

The day I drove over to check the place out, it felt abandoned. Everything seemed desolate, as if the ghosts of those sixteen skydivers still haunted the airfield. None of the staff members were very enthusiastic, but I'd driven all the way over so I decided to get my money's worth by taking their five-dollar promotional flight. The cheap price was just a marketing hook, and in my case, it worked. That very day I signed up for flight lessons.

The first few flights were okay, but after that I started feeling claustrophobic. I wanted to taste and feel the sky, not just gaze at it through a wall of plastic. Flying in a plane made me feel like Superman wearing an iron lung. I wanted more.

A few days later, I read an article in the Cleveland *Plain Dealer* about a guy who'd just designed a miniature helicopter called a Bensen Gyrocopter. It had a VW motor, a wooden propeller on the back, and tricycle gear for landing. With a helicopter blade on top and a seat made of tubular aluminum, it resembled a flying lawn chair.

You could actually put one of these things together for $1,500, which sounded to me like a fair price for such a funky toy. The article said the gyrocopter was currently on display at the Cleveland Sportsman's Show, so I hurried down to have a look.

I happily wandered around the show until one particular sign caught my eye through the colorful maze of booths. It said *Cleveland School of Sport Parachuting,* and below it a small crowd had gathered to watch a slide presentation of people in free fall. As I stepped closer and closer to the awesome images, I heard someone ask, "Are you interested in skydiving? Can I help you?"

Standing beside me was a very tan guy in a jump suit with a big smile and a brochure in his hand. I could tell he was gearing up for the sales pitch, but I saved him the trouble by asking, "Where do I sign up?" I forgot all about the gyro-copter!

Just a few days later, I was on my way to an airfield lo-cated in the beautiful Amish country of Garrettsville, Ohio. I drove way out on Route 82 until I spotted a dirt runway filled with Cessnas and an assortment of long metal buildings. Then I got out of the car, meandered into the office and an-nounced, "I'm Mickey Robinson, and I'm jumping today."

In the next five minutes, a female instructor guided me up a stepladder and buckled me into a military T-10 harness suspended from the ceiling beam of the clubhouse. I felt a little like a Peking duck, hanging there while she spieled out a brief overview of skydiving.

Next she showed me how to pull up on the risers so I could pretend I was actually operating and steering the bulky T-10 parachute. This was a perfect chute for beginners, and they'd made its operation practically foolproof.

When it came time to jump out of the plane, my body weight would actually pull the ripcord and extract the chute automatically. Even if I froze in midair, the chute would open.

I was so excited that everything became a detailed blur as she rattled on for three hours about various malfunctions and emergency procedures. But I remembered the important things: how to deploy my reserve parachute by opening it and throwing it out; how to count 1,000, 2,000, then look at the dummy ripcord and pull on 3,000; and how to exit the plane and position myself for free fall.

Wearing a giant crash helmet and black goggles, I looked like a mutant fly as I hopped aboard the little Cessna 180. I shook hands with the pilot, Dale, and then excitedly settled into my seat as we began our climb to 2,800 feet. I noticed Dale's voice became strangely calm as he slowed the plane down to 80 miles per hour, reached across my chest and said, "Now I'm gonna open the door."

All of a sudden I felt like a little kid being strapped into a roller coaster. Dale kept telling me everything he was doing so I wouldn't panic, but panic was the farthest thing from my mind.

As the door opened a half-mile above the earth, I felt a sweet, cool rush of heavenly wind. Unable to hear anything but the hypnotic drone of the engine, I gazed down at the amazing patchwork quilt of Amish countryside. It was the most beautiful sight I'd ever seen, and the smell of the wind made it doubly intoxicating.

For a brief moment I was lost in space, but then I remembered I was supposed to jump out of the plane. I snapped out of my stupor, reached out the open door, grabbed hold of the wing strut and pulled myself onto the welded steel step. I couldn't help but notice the wing strut was almost stripped of paint from all the scratch marks made by human fingernails.

Dale alternately looked out his window and then back at me to determine the right spot to let me out. As I waited for his signal, I playfully kicked my leg into the air like a Rockette. It felt a little like hanging out of a car window while joy riding on a Saturday night.

When Dale finally found the spot, he slapped me on the leg and yelled, "Okay—Go!" As I pushed off, I put my arms and legs out just the way I'd been taught. Instantly I heard this deafening Whooooooooosssshhh. Then perfect silence.

The quiet was unbelievable. As the scenery whizzed past me like a speeding train, I tried to remember what I was supposed to do next.

Just then I felt a slow tug followed by a sharp jerk. Instantly I was suspended beneath this olive-drab canopy, hanging quietly above the earth like a little herald angel in a Christmas play. All I could see above me was a huge dark circle with a little bit of blue shining through a 12-inch hole at the center. But when I looked down, I was overwhelmed. I felt like I was driving the winning chariot in *Ben-Hur*— except my horses weren't made of flesh and blood. They were made of air.

Then I noticed my feet floating so small and helplessly above the huge green earth. Ohio looked perfect from up here, and no one was in a hurry. Cars and trucks and people were all moving at the humble and gentle speed of a snail.

Drifting in a sky-blue daydream, I momentarily forgot that I was falling to earth. But the instructors had planned for that. A person could be unconscious and still land in the right spot with the T-10 parachute. As I neared the 100-acre field where I was to land, I heard a deep voice booming out of nowhere, filling the sky around me.

"Okay, Mickey, you're looking great. You're coming right in. Keep your eyes on the horizon."

They'd rigged up a P.A. system in order to remind first-timers that the ground was an essential part of the jump.

In the last few seconds, beginners have a tendency to look down and pull their legs up. Just as I was considering doing that, the voice on the loudspeaker said, "Keep your eyes on the horizon, Mickey. Pull up on the risers, and get your feet together."

I obediently pulled my feet together, but couldn't resist looking down. The eternity of the sky instantly slammed shut as the ground came keenly into focus. Feeling a sharp jolt, I tumbled softly and it was over. In less than 4½ minutes, *Ben-Hur* disappeared and Mickey Robinson took his place. I felt joyful and hyper, but desperate to do it again.

After a moment of congratulations from my instructor, everyone disappeared. To them this was business as usual, but I was lit up like a Roman candle. Since no one was sticking around to share my ecstasy, I dutifully followed Dale into the clubhouse to sign my name in the little logbook. It's customary for the pilot to sign off by marking the date, altitude and a few comments about the jump.

I felt like a kid who's dying to ride the roller coaster one more time, but this was Dale's last load of the day. I could tell he was ready to head for home, yet he kindly took the time to offer me a shot of whiskey and a parting cigarette. As he signed off the paperwork, I asked, "What's next?"

Most people make one jump and are never heard from again. Only one out of ten ever return for a second jump, and the ones who become skydivers are rarer still. But I knew, without a doubt, I was coming back.

"Well, Mickey, we've got this package deal," he explained. "You get seven jumps for $100, and by the sixth jump, you're in free fall. How does that sound?"

"Sign me up!" I beamed.

On the way home I kept shouting, "Yes!" at the top of my lungs while honking the horn and picking up speed. I'd finally found it! Skydiving was better than Julie. Better than career options. Better than money. I would become a skydiving evangelist, ready to convert the lost, the stupid and the bored to the greatest thrill on earth. Skydiving was the single most liberating thrill for me, and it provided a false sense of freedom from the mundane in this world.

But I was about to discover that people weren't exactly responsive to my zeal. After awhile, my friends starting rolling their eyes and telling me to shut up. But that didn't stop me. I was a man with a vision! Julie's absence and a dead-end job didn't bother me anymore, as long as I knew that airfield was waiting for me at the end of the day.

I advanced rapidly through the first five jumps, and three weeks later I experienced my first free fall. I jumped from the plane, immediately made a big X with my body and became stable in half a second. I felt like a leaf drifting down from a tree as I counted 1,000, 2,000, then looked directly at the rectangular ring, reaching for it and pulling on the count of 3,000.

The brilliant red T-U parachute slid easily out of its pack, unlike the bulky T-10, and exploded above me. I was no longer restricted, but could now pull on the steering lines and actually maneuver in the sky.

That day I maneuvered myself a little too far out of the drop zone and landed in the woods. But I didn't care—any more than Lindbergh cared that he was a few miles off on his first transatlantic flight.

I somehow fumbled the parachute into my arms before sitting silently on a log to savor the moment. I couldn't move. I was numb with peace. I'd just experienced baptism . . . breakaway . . . the true beginning! I was born for the sky, and now I passionately embraced it—body, mind, soul and spirit.

I quickly immersed myself in the skydiving culture and became fluent in its language. Terms like *free fall, relative work* and *dead center* became part of my working vocabulary. All I ever thought about was skydiving. When I'd wake up in the morning and look out the window, my first thought would be, "Is this a good day for a jump?"

Although my world was still mostly black and white, it turned a radiant technicolor when I stepped onto that runway.

The day finally arrived when I could no longer endure the thought of gas grills, so I got my old job back at Otis Elevator. My new co-workers were friendly enough, but they couldn't relate to my obsession. When I tried to describe the wonders of free fall, I received everything from smiles to scorn.

"You think you're cool now that you're a skydiver?"

"Sounds good, Mickey. I wish I could try something like that."

"I've got a wife and kids to support. I can't throw money away like you single guys."

It only cost me $3.50 a jump, but I was jumping as often as possible, so my expenses were beginning to stack up like shot glasses on St. Patrick's Day. My worldly possessions consisted of a car, ski equipment and clothes, but I didn't care about those things anymore. All I wanted was skydiving gear.

I heard about a guy who'd broken his hip and was retiring from the sport, so I ending up buying his red, white and blue Paracommander parachute. Then I ordered special boots and a white jumpsuit with elastic sewn around the wrists, neck and ankles. Although I'd never placed much value on material possessions, these items quickly became sacred to me.

Purchasing my own gear was like receiving vestments for ordination. I was now able to participate in the ritual of worshipping what I loved above all else. I was ready to take my vows as a priest of the sky.

Chapter Ten

What Goes Up . . .

One rainy day in July, I was inside the clubhouse packing my parachute when a guy I'd never seen before came strolling in. I couldn't take my eyes off him as he walked up and tossed a flexible metal tube onto the table in front of me.

It was the tube that holds the parachute ripcord, and I could see it had a little stone wedged just inside the opening. He flashed me a wry smile as he pointed to it and said, "If anybody asks, that's pea gravel."

He was referring to the ball-bearing-shaped stones that cover the small area skydivers call the *ground target*. This fastest-gun-in-the-West guy was actually saying to me, "I always land dead center." Just as I was trying to think of an intelligent comeback, he abruptly turned and walked out the door.

"Who *is* that guy?" I asked.

"That's Dan," said a pilot standing nearby. "He's D-44." (This meant he was the 44th person in the United States to qualify for the top license in skydiving).

"How come I've never seen this guy Dan around the drop zone before?"

"He wracked up on a jump, so he's been out for awhile," said the pilot with a knowing grin. "Dan's always getting hurt. He's the last of the Mohicans."

From that day on, Dan became the man to watch. I thought of him as a skydiving guru, but in actuality he was just a forty-five-year-old Irish Catholic who liked to drink whiskey and jump out of airplanes.

While growing up tough in a poor Cleveland neighborhood, Dan had fallen in love with danger and it turned out to be a lifelong romance. Employed as an iron worker, Dan liked climbing to the top of skyscrapers and walking out on six-inch beams so he could catch a bird's-eye view of the city.

Although he swore like a sailor and drank like a fish, he never jumped out of an airplane without making the sign of the cross. Dan thrived on show jumps and relative work, but he wasn't a show-off. He didn't care about reputation. He just loved free fall.

By this time, I was jumping at 7,500 feet, which gave me thirty seconds of free fall. That doesn't sound like much, but each second peeled another layer off my five senses until I felt totally awake and totally alive.

As I fell into that huge hammock of clouds, I instantly began to stretch and turn and make myself comfortable in the sky. As I twisted and arched my body, I was elated to find I could zoom through the air two feet horizontally for every vertical foot I fell.

With every jump, I was becoming more and more sensitive to time and distance. My eyes began letting me know just how far I was above the earth while my brain ticked off seconds as accurately as a Swiss watch. I instinctively knew not to trust altimeters and watches. All the best skydivers relied on an inner knowing of what to do and when to do it, and I was going to be one of the best.

As I got more and more comfortable with free fall, I couldn't wait to make contact in relative work. In this deceptively simple-looking maneuver, the first person, called a pin man, jumps and falls stable in a fixed position until the next skydiver can fly over to him and make contact.

The second jumper has to increase his speed at first and then slow down in order to mesh with the pin man. Although it looks easy, it's entirely possible for unskilled skydivers to overshoot or crash into each other. Although I tried it with a couple of different people, each time was a disappointment.

We looked like kids trying to grab each other's butt rather than skilled skydivers trying to execute a difficult maneuver.

After one botched attempt, Dan walked up to me and said, "I hear you're having a problem making contact."

"Well . . . yeah . . . I . . . "

"You wanna make contact?" he interrupted. "Come with me."

He didn't wait for an answer, but turned on his heel and walked into the clubhouse. I could hardly believe it. Dan was inviting me to jump with him. That was like Gary Cooper asking me to be his deputy.

Dusk had begun to fall the evening Dan and I took off for our first jump together, but the sun had not yet set at 10,000 feet.

"What I want you to do is fall stable and find something big to look at, like a barn," Dan explained, as our plane climbed into the brilliant summer sky. "Keep your eye on that thing, make the biggest X you can, go as slow as you can, and wait. I'll be there."

I went off the step nearly two miles above the earth, fell in a perfect X, and then spotted a big white barn three or four miles away. Remembering Dan's advice, I aimed for it and didn't move even one degree to the right or left. With arms outstretched and hands cupped, I tried to grab as much air as I possibly could. Falling straight and slow, I heard the now familiar sound of my body dropping through space . . . SSShhhhooowwhhhooosh.

Suddenly I felt a tug on my ankle, and as my body spun sharply around, two strong hands grasped my wrists and pulled me to within eight inches of Dan's grinning face. At that exact moment, he welcomed me into the brotherhood of the sky. I was being initiated into a secret society, and it felt religious, like God touching Adam.

I was no longer alone with the clouds and the earth and the air. I had made contact with another human being. That changed everything, and I suddenly understood why Dan loved relative work. Free fall was too awesome, too sacred, not to be shared.

As we neared "opening altitude" of 2,000 feet, Dan and I pushed away from each other like separating spacecraft. I lifted my upper body to track in the opposite direction and, when I was well away from Dan, waved my arms above my head before pulling the ripcord. As the red Paracommander billowed out, it jerked and spun me around just in time to catch Dan's last second of free fall.

For a split second, it looked as if I went rocketing toward heaven while he continued hurtling toward earth. As the sky swallowed his solitary figure, I saw for the first time, from the sky, what a man looked like free falling at 125 miles per hour.

Then I saw a tiny poof as Dan's chute opened and he began to bob gently in the sky like a red lure on blue water. As I watched him in the distance, I felt so proud to be his friend.

It was almost dark by the time we landed, and I was like a little kid on the fourth of July. Abuzz with elation, all I wanted to do was stay close to this man. After tossing our gear into the back of the car, we drove up to a little country bar where skydivers relived their greatness and got totally looped.

"Okay, Mickey, let me show you how it's done," explained Dan while stepping up to the bar and lifting an impressively large beer mug. "Here's to Cardinal Puff for the first time." Then he took a long swig of beer and proceeded to tap on the bar six times before saying, "Here's to Cardinal Puff for the second time," taking another swig.

When I caught a glimpse of myself in the mirror over the bar, I was grinning from ear to ear. Everything about this guy was larger-than-life. Dan was a hero even when he drank, and hanging out in a bar with him was a whole lot different than hanging out with my dad.

Amidst the clanking of glasses and the smoking of cigarettes, Dan continued undaunted. He was single-minded even when it came to this silly game. He and I played on, consuming huge quantities of beer, tapping the bar incessantly with our fingers and making many runs to the bathroom.

Due to some kind of superhuman tolerance for alcohol, Dan was able to complete the game without making a mistake, and this awarded him the dubious but distinctive title of "Pope." I believe Dan was one of the few skydivers who ever made it to that level without passing out.

I was bleary-eyed when we finally called it a night, but Dan seemed amazingly sober as we drove back to the airport. As I grabbed my stuff out of the trunk, he yelled over his shoulder, "Same time tomorrow night?"

"Huh? Sure! Anytime!" Dan was letting me in. The door of the inner circle was finally swinging open in my direction.

Dan and I went on to make many, many jumps together, and ultimately he asked me to become part of his demo team, The Red Eagles. That was the greatest honor I'd ever received. Even though Dan was a legendary maverick in the sport, he was incredibly respected. This man had survived more than his share of disasters and had even escaped drowning on that ill-fated jump over Lake Erie.

Dan had planned to go up that day, but at the last minute he had to bow out because of an injury. His partner, Richie, jumped without him, and rescue teams later found Richie's body only 100 yards from shore. He had somehow managed to swim that far in full gear before his heart finally burst from exhaustion. Although Richie's death hit Dan pretty hard, it didn't stop him. Nothing could keep that man out of the sky for very long.

After Dan took me on as his disciple, my star rose rapidly. The other guys began to notice my existence, and it wasn't long before I started getting offers to take part in show jumps for political functions and church carnivals.

On those hot summer days, I would stroll through the crowd of onlookers in my white jumpsuit while consuming large quantities of hot dogs and beer. I was especially good at impressing all the female fans, and soon I earned the nickname *Superstar*.

I belonged to the elite group of athletes who talked non-stop about women, free fall, competition and themselves. I quickly learned there was a caste system to this sport, and its supreme being was known as the National Champion. In the unwritten rules of our manifesto, no one was allowed to speak to him unless he spoke to you first.

I also learned that most skydivers believed in nothing but themselves. Some would even blaspheme and mock God before jumping off the step. These were young, healthy world-class athletes who lived off adrenalin and pride. Their religion was free fall and their altar was the sky. Beyond that, nothing mattered.

But Dan was different. This man was no saint, but neither was he a blasphemer. Dan steadfastly believed there was a God to be reckoned with, and I liked that about him. Both of us were exiles from the church, yet both of us had been forever marked by the fear and wonder of a Catholic childhood.

One day in mid-August, a guy named Doug walked up to me after a jump and said, "You really ought to consider competition." I recognized him as one of the elite, and I'd heard he was getting ready to take a stunt-jumping team to a Labor Day exhibition in Wisconsin.

"Let me tell you about Wisconsin, Mickey," he said enthusiastically. "Free water-skiing, free food, plenty of females and five jumps a day."

"No way! I'd give anything to do that!"

"Why don't you plan on coming with us next summer?"

"Yeah, count me in. I'll be ready."

I drove over to see my old friend Pete that night to smoke a joint and tell him about my big opportunity. Pete had just recently returned from Vietnam, carrying with him a pair of old army boots stuffed with marijuana.

Although I'd known the guy since high school, I started to feel kind of uneasy around him. Pete had become strangely cynical, especially about America, but he wouldn't talk about Vietnam. In fact, he never wanted to talk about anything anymore. All he wanted to do was hang out in the basement and get stoned.

Once in awhile I'd drive over to smoke a joint with him, and he'd halfheartedly listen while I talked about free fall, Dan, and the national champion. But Pete was in a really weird mood that night.

At one point, he lifted my parachute pack off the couch, took a hit off the joint and then murmured under his breath, "Is this what you use when you crash?"

When he said those words, I felt something cold trickle down my spine. "That's kinda weird, Pete. Sounds like you're putting bad luck on me or something."

"No, man. Just stands to reason. Flyboys gotta hit the ground sometime."

The drugs and conversation were making me feel uneasy. "I gotta go, Pete. I gotta get some sleep. We're trying out Walt's new plane tomorrow."

As I walked to the door and opened it, Pete called out, "Hey, Mickey."

When I turned, I could barely see his face through the haze of dimly lit smoke. For a split second, Pete looked like the Cheshire cat, sitting there on the couch smoking his hookah and grinning at me from out of the darkness.

"What?" I barked, more than ready to get out of there.

"It's just gravity, man. What goes up must come down."

Little did I know. Life as I knew it would be drastically changed—never to be the same again.

Chapter Eleven

All Fall Down

As the ambulance sped through the night, I whispered the prayer of contrition through what was left of my mouth: *"Oh my God, I am heartily sorry for having offended thee . . . "*

When we jolted to a stop, the doors exploded open and paramedics slid me out as smoothly as bread from the oven.

"I detest all my sins because of Thy just punishment, but most of all because they offend Thee . . . "

Wheeling me from the silent darkness into the blinding light of emergency, they descended on me like ants attacking an injured sparrow. As pieces of my jumpsuit were cut away, I heard a voice say, "Third-degree burns covering 35 percent of his body."

Something sharp slid into my left hand as soaking wet towels covered my arms and legs. I watched a vast network of tubes crisscross above me as a nurse peeled the melted sock from my right foot.

"Oh Lord, who art all good and worthy of all my love."

"This guy is a mess. Did somebody call his family?"

"I firmly resolve, with the help of Thy grace, to sin no more and to avoid the near occasion of sin."

"Forget family. Better call a priest."

"Amen."

My mother was at work when she received the phone call.

"Is this Jean Robinson?"

"Yes?"

"Your son, Mickey, has been injured in a plane crash. Please come immediately to the admissions desk at Southwest General in Berea."

Julie was working at her summer job when she picked up the phone and heard my mother's frantic voice.

"Mickey's plane crashed. We've got to go to the hospital right away. He's hurt real bad."

"Is he . . .?"

"No! He's gonna be okay."

They wouldn't let Julie in, but my mother was allowed to see me for 60 seconds. Although heavily dosed with morphine, I whispered, "Don't blame skydiving, Mom." Like a zealot singing hymns while being burned at the stake, I was ready to defend my religion to the grave.

Almost delirious, I insisted that my mother find Father John. I didn't want to die until I received last rites from a priest. By some miracle, my mother was able to locate the man who'd terrorized my Catholic boyhood. Although he'd long since retired from St. Michael's, Father John mercifully drove to the hospital that night to anoint me for burial.

This time he didn't scare me. His once-booming voice sounded soft and far away as he began the rite of extreme unction: *"Per istam sanctam unctionem (Through this holy anointing)."*

The ancient prayer called me back from behind the heavy curtain of shock. I didn't know what the Latin words meant, but they penetrated to a place far beyond hearing.

"...et suam piissimam misericordiam indulgeat tibi Dominus quidquid deliquisti (may the Lord forgive you whatever sins you have committed)."

Then Father John dipped his huge thumb into the tiny vial of holy oil and lightly touched the charred remains of my eyes, nose, lips, ears and hands. I remembered my catechism. Whatever sins I'd committed through these five senses had now been covered by the forgiving hand of God.

Father John had barely finished his prayer when they wheeled me down an echoing hallway into a room filled with pain. The nurses immediately pulled a curtain around me so I couldn't see the other patients, but I knew they were there. I could hear and feel groaning all around me.

This was the Intensive Care Unit, a place where human beings lay in the twilight between life and death. The doctor had determined that I wouldn't survive being transported to the first-class burn center at Brook Army Medical Center in Texas. So they kept me at Southwest General Community Hospital. Little did I know that this place would be my home for many nights to come.

Although this hospital was hardly prepared for a disaster like me, the staff tried their best to keep me from dying. Pumping fluid into my body seemed as useless as watering a dead tree. Still, the nurses fluttered in every fifteen minutes to rotate IV bottles and cover me with wet towels.

Throughout the night I'd doze off and then wake up, hoping it was all a nightmare. But the pain would mercilessly jerk me back to reality. Almost half of my nineteen-year-old body was now a black, oozing wound. Even though I was barely conscious, a phrase kept repeating itself over and over in my mind: "God, I'm sorry! I want to live! Please give me another chance."

The pain was so excruciating, I felt like I'd been dropped into a live volcano. Lying helplessly on my back and unable to move, I remembered a movie I'd seen once where people in togas were buried under molten lava. Not many things scared me when I was a kid, but the thought of being burned alive haunted me. I thought that would be the grossest possible way to go. Except, those people in Pompeii mercifully died within seconds.

I was still alive.

According to the doctors, I was so near death they waived many restrictions, allowing special friends and family to visit me. Still, they excluded my father, deciding that seeing him might upset me. So Dad was banished from my bedside.

No one was really prepared for what they saw upon entering ICU that morning after the crash. I didn't look human anymore. In addition to the horrendous burns, my head had swollen to twice its normal size, and some people nearly fainted after taking one look at me.

When I finally opened my eyes that first morning, my friend Bob was staring down at me with an anguished look on his face. He'd somehow gotten in through the hospital laundry, then snuck up to my room when no one was looking.

"How ya' doin', Mickey?" he whispered softly.

"I don't know."

"Don't you worry, Mick. Italians die damn hard."

The nurses had injected me with so much morphine, I was totally out of it. When one of my co-workers came to visit later that day, I just stared blankly at him and said, "What're you doing here? Why aren't you at work?"

Nothing was real to me except pain. Night after night, the doctors expected me to die before morning, but I miraculously outlived their prognosis. Still, it took incredible effort just to keep what was left of my body from rotting away. Every two hours, the nurses had to wrap my burned legs in clean towels and soak them with silver nitrate to try to kill the infection.

My right hand was so raw and mangled, the doctor recommended amputation. With veins sticking out and fingers melted together, it was burned into a tightly clenched fist. The nurses ingeniously rigged up a plastic bag to put in the bed with me, filled it with a silver nitrate/saline solution, and then stuck my hand in it to soak.

But the most dreaded part of every day was *debridement,* a strangely innocent word describing a procedure probably invented by Nazis. I distinctly remember the first time I ever heard that word. It was the day a doctor came to cut parts of my face off.

Since dead tissue was fertile ground for infection, pieces of morbid flesh had to be removed on a daily basis. One day a doctor strolled in all nice and friendly, followed by a very efficient-looking nurse carrying a tray full of steel instruments.

"Hello, Mr. Robinson. How're you feeling? We're here to do a little cleanup on you today."

Then he nonchalantly reached for a pair of scissors and pinchers, like a sculptor getting ready to carve a statue— except I wasn't made of marble. As he started working on my burned ear, I heard a crunching sound. I began to feel nauseous, but I didn't utter a word of protest.

I thought I was supposed to take it like a man, but I didn't feel like a man anymore. Everything I thought made me a normal human being had been taken away.

I had lost all my physical functions and my friends. I had been stripped down to the lowest level of human survival: consciousness, emotions, and extreme pain.

After several weeks, I was still failing to respond to anything the doctors attempted to do. At that point, they called in a highly respected specialist from a major hospital for consultation. After a thorough examination, the specialist described my condition in amazingly complex terms. But his concluding statement was easy to understand. "There is nothing I have to offer this young man."

So the ministers of medicine gave me up to die. But there was one element that wasn't in the diagnosis—the God factor. Although my vital signs looked hopeless, something in me was determined to live. The doctors didn't understand this, and I couldn't blame them for their ignorance. Even I didn't begin to comprehend the vast difference between *body* and *spirit* until the day my sister's father-in-law came to visit me.

Dr. Jeric was a civilian who'd just returned from thirteen months of voluntary duty in Vietnam. He'd worked on dozens of burn victims over there and he wanted to see if there was anything he could do to help me.

Walking into my hospital room, Dr. Jeric took one look and thought, *No way!* He'd seen soldiers in Vietnam die from less serious burns than mine. Still, he sat down by my bed and encouraged me to fight for life. When he was ready to leave, I stood to my feet and walked him down the hall.

"Thank you for coming to see me," I said.

But he didn't respond.

"How long do you think it'll be before I'm able to go home?"

Once again, he didn't respond. That was odd. Didn't he hear me?

I stood there with him as the ICU door began opening automatically. Then it happened. As if I was a ghost, the door swung right through me.

In the next second, my spirit was drawn back into my body like a rubber band being snapped. As I lay there trying to understand what just happened, I realized a part of me was hovering between this world and the next.

But why?

Just a few days later, I took a drastic turn for the worse. As my fever soared to 106, I was sure I could hear the sound of my own blood boiling.

Infections raged throughout my body, especially in my right hand, which the doctors wanted to amputate. I had lost a tremendous amount of fluid and was rapidly losing weight. I was blind in one eye and huge bedsores were consuming what was left of my flesh. Poisonous microorganisms swarmed through my blood. I was in mind-bending pain.

My nervous system was so sensitive that if someone so much as brushed against the bed, I felt like they'd hit me with a sledgehammer. Although my fever was dangerously high, the nurses didn't dare pack my body in ice or rub me with alcohol because I was a piece of raw meat.

So they placed a vinyl sheet underneath me and began pumping refrigerated fluid through a network of tubes under my body. Now I was burning up on the inside while freezing on the outside, shivering and shaking so violently that the metal bars on my bed clanged against the wall.

My body was like a switchbox, and the switches were shutting down one at a time. That's when the doctor called my sister Barbara. "You'd better come in this morning," he said. "I don't think he'll be here by my afternoon rounds."

My brother also came that day to stand faithfully at the foot of my bed while I swam in and out of consciousness. With only one good eye, I squinted hard, trying to focus on his face. But as I stared straight ahead, a strange picture began forming right next to him. Hanging there in midair was the scene of a long white room with rows and rows of pathology tables.

"Where am I?" I asked out loud. "Did they move me?"

He looked at me strangely. "What're you talking about, Mickey?"

Suddenly I knew where I was.

"We're in the morgue," I said matter-of-factly, too sick to be afraid.

With a look of confusion and concern on his face, he said, "You're okay, Mickey."

I wasn't delirious. In fact, I was thinking more clearly than I had since the accident. I distinctly remember the shirt my brother was wearing, and I was fully aware of every word he was saying.

Then, as mysteriously as it had appeared, the scene of the morgue slowly vanished. But at the same time, like a butterfly emerging from a cocoon, something strong and alive stepped out of my broken body. My legs sank down through the mattress as my spirit rose to its feet, sweeping through flesh as gently as wings sweep through air.

Instantly, I left behind tremendous pain and a burning fever to enter another realm—a realm not ruled by natural law. Gravity ceased and time stopped as eternity swung open before me like a garden gate.

Chapter Twelve

Spirit in the Sky

Colors suddenly pulsated with brilliance, as if misted by a fine morning rain. Objects loomed into view with razor-sharp clarity, as if I was seeing them for the first time. I felt more purely alive than on the happiest day of my childhood. And when I looked down to see my mangled hand, it was perfect.

Instantly, I knew this was the real world. The eternal world.

All I'd ever known had been imprisoned by time. But in this realm of spirit, there was no such thing as yesterday or tomorrow.

Everything that had been would always be.

My human understanding of *time* just wasn't important anymore. Even my thoughts were no longer based upon the sum of my experience. Before I even conceived a question, the answer resonated within me, and this knowing came as a gift, not as an exercise.

I felt like a creature who'd always lived at the bottom of the sea in shadow and silence. Now I was swimming upward in waves of light and sound, bursting through the surface with an awareness far beyond logic or reasoning.

With relentless but gentle speed, I began traveling toward a pure white light, brighter than a thousand suns. I could gaze forever and ever into the wonderful light.

But, then, as my whole being yearned for this brilliance, I became aware of something moving in behind me. Like a child being put to bed in a strange room, I felt an eerie blackness hovering. Then, as if someone was closing a door in front of me, the amazing light began shrinking into a mere sliver.

The darkness that encompassed me was something more terrifying than evil. This was total emptiness waiting to penetrate and swallow all that made me alive. And I was helpless, totally incapable of saving myself.

Realizing I was about to be separated from the light, I experienced an agony more terrible than being burned alive. I knew if the darkness swallowed me, I would be imprisoned in an empty world with no windows and no door. I would cry for help, yet never be heard.

Dreams of being and doing would become nightmares of frustration. Any longing for love or passionate embrace would be answered by aloneness. And this aloneness would be final. Non-negotiable. Never ending. Forever.

Shivering in terror, I watched the last eclipse of light disappearing. Then, like a drowning man gasping for air, my spirit screamed out the same words I'd prayed that night in Intensive Care: "God, I'm sorry! I want to live! Please give me another chance!"

These words came straight from my heart, focused and sharp, like arrows seeking a target. And just as they escaped my lips, I found myself standing in heaven.

Instantly, the darkness retreated and a living, breathing glory enfolded me. This glory was not just a feeling or an emotion . . . it was a presence. And although I could not see any form or shape, I knew it was a Person.

The magnificence of this Person pierced me like a laser. Forever to the east and forever to the west radiated all Power, all Wisdom, all Splendor, all Love. I was at the center of a shooting star! I was an ice cube melting in a sea of light.

I no longer cared about skydiving, Julie, my body, my life. Nothing mattered anymore. Nothing mattered except to remain in this Presence. I didn't know whether I was dead or alive, but if I was dead, I wanted to stay dead!

Love drenched me like a flood, and no drug high or adrenalin rush could compare with what I was experiencing. I was being filled with Life itself, consuming my aloneness.

I was no longer the finite, singular being known as Mickey Robinson. The umbilical cord of my spirit was linked to my Creator, and I vibrated in His presence like a human tuning fork. There was no such thing as fear. No such thing as sorrow. No such thing as emptiness.

I was fully alive! I was infinite.

And I was no longer alone.

I never saw a face, or a throne, or heard choirs of angels. But with arms outstretched, I breathed in the radiance of this pure being clothed in perfect light. And as I rested in the certainty of this Presence, a vision began to unfold.

Something like supernatural television flashed random scenes from the next seven years of my life. While some images focused slowly and painstakingly, others rushed past me like speeding cars on a freeway. Specific seconds, minutes, hours, days, and even weeks were mysteriously plucked out of sequence and shown to me in this divine version of virtual reality.

The first scenes were heart wrenching. I watched young kids sticking needles into their arms and even into their stomachs as the drug scene exploded throughout America. And woven into these tragic film clips were images of Mickey Robinson doing stupid things—wrong things.

When these appeared, I would scream out helplessly, "No! Don't do that!" But the film never stopped. It just rolled on relentlessly as I stood there, like Ebenezer Scrooge, fully awake and full of remorse for my wrong actions.

Then I was no longer a spectator. When the film clips suddenly ended, I found myself standing in front of my brother, but there was something wrong. He had an eerie and vacant expression on his face. I tried talking to him but he just stared blankly at me. In total frustration, I cried out, "I can't get through to him!"

Then the scene shifted as his face slowly disappeared. I found myself standing in a grassy yard on a warm spring day, facing a rusty gate that opened onto a narrow path. I could smell the sweet perfume of lilacs as a young woman walked toward me. I didn't recognize her face, but I knew her. She was somehow part of me, and so was this place.

Then, heaviness filled me as I stared at some driftwood lying by my feet. Ocean waves crashed in the distance as I looked up and saw a strange man walking toward me. As he came closer, I knew I was in danger and had to run away as fast as I could.

Then the heavy feeling disappeared as the scene shifted one last time. I was walking down a steep mountain path overlooking a sapphire sea. There were several people in front of me, laughing and enjoying the beauty of this sun-drenched day. The lush smell of tropical flowers and fruit was so intoxicating, I heard myself say, "So this is paradise!"

Just as I said the word *paradise,* the vision ended. God then revealed to me, through His Spirit, that He was sending me back. Gently, He tugged me back to earth, even as a kite would be reeled in.

I was caught in a cosmic birth canal, sliding irresistibly into another dimension, yet I didn't want to leave the womb of eternity. I didn't want to leave His Presence. I was being carried from one world into another by the breath of God.

But suddenly, the glory faded as I sank back into my body, like a sparkling diamond sinking into mud. Instead of the wonderful light, I was now gazing up at a gray ventilation shaft on the ICU ceiling.

Slowly, objects began materializing around me, but everything looked blurred and shadowy, as if covered by a thin gauze veil. Someone was speaking a language I'd never heard before, so I couldn't make out any words. The crystalline tones of eternity had now been replaced by the muffled and static sounds of earth.

I wondered who was speaking, and what was he saying?

Then I realized my lips were moving. The strange words were pouring out of me! But this thought barely registered before I began drifting off again. My fever had broken, and

Mickey at 5
years of age.

Mickey at 18
years old / 1967.

Disaster;
the once pretty
jump aircraft.

The aftermath of
August 15th, 1968,
plane crash

A long
long climb
ahead...

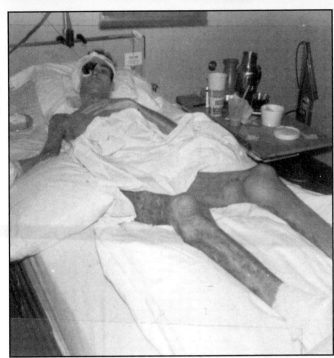

...on burned
and nerve
damaged
legs.

They said I'd
never walk!

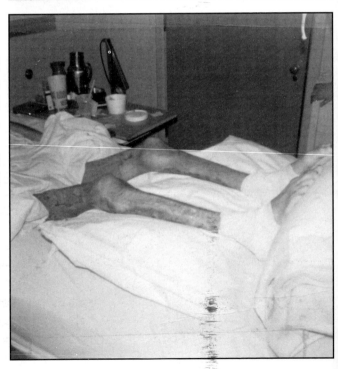

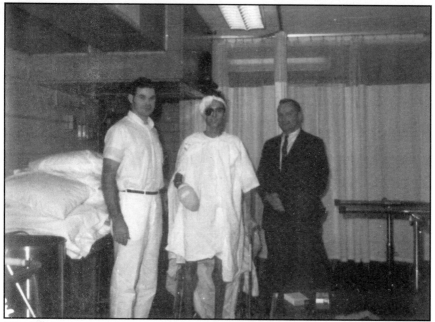

That's "one small step for man"...

Psalm 40:2
"He also brought me up out of a horrible pit, Out of the miry clay, And set my feet upon a rock, And established my steps." / New Brunswick, Canada

Barbara and I on the farm with Michael and Matthew / 1978

Back Row; Barbara and I, Elizabeth and Michael
Up front: Jacob and Matthew; all at home in Franklin, Tennessee

Barbara and I, through it all, together for 30 years! Praise God! Amen!

for the first time since the accident, I fell into the mercy of a deep, natural sleep.

Chapter Thirteen

Just Barely Alive

I was floating in a tranquil sea. Nothing could disturb me—so great was the peace I owned. Although I could vaguely hear voices coming from outside the calm, I ignored them. But when I heard a sharp metal *CLANG*, I reluctantly opened one eye and discovered several human shapes surrounding my bed. The room was painfully bright, yet the faces staring down at me were dark.

I was still tuned to the frequency of heaven, but these people were on a whole different channel. *What is wrong with everybody?* I wondered to myself. *Why are they so bummed out?*

These doctors and nurses looked like they were getting ready to roll me into cold storage. Didn't they know I was alive? I wanted to sit up and show them, but I quickly discovered it was impossible to move. I had no strength at all. Besides, the feverish sweat had dried and glued me firmly to the sheets. My body was now embalmed in its own fluid, encased within a tight, stinking shroud.

Yet I'd never felt so alive! I didn't want to breathe for fear that I would expel the air of heaven from my lungs. Although every second threatened to pull me further and further from where I'd been, I clutched peace the way a child clutches his pillow after an amazing dream. If I didn't move, if I didn't breathe, if I didn't speak—maybe it would never go away.

Then I overheard one of the doctors speaking sharply to a nurse, and the *sound* of his words made me cringe. For some reason, I was now *extraordinarily sensitive*. Even the slightest expression of conflict fell on me like acid rain. I'd been in the presence of God, and just as the flames had once swept over my body, divine love now swept through me like a holy wind.

"Welcome back," said one of the doctors as he looked up from his clipboard. "We didn't know if we'd be seeing you again, Mr. Robinson. How are you feeling?"

I couldn't answer. My brain couldn't form words powerful enough to describe how I was feeling. The doctors and nurses probably interpreted my silence as a symptom of pain, so they politely filed out of the room and left me alone with the peace.

The peace was all I had to hold onto. Even though a candle had been lit in the darkness of my spirit, I was still ravaged on the outside. I would have to cling to the memory of heaven in order to survive the painful hours, days, weeks, months and years that lay ahead.

While lying on that bed in Intensive Care, drifting in and out of consciousness, my rigid body defied my mind and began to curl into a fetal position. The nurses were supposed to turn me regularly to maintain my circulation, but they probably felt it was a waste of time because of the severity of my condition. As a result, huge bedsores formed on the left side of my body, and fist-sized pieces of rotting flesh soon covered my hip and buttock.

I was no longer considered *terminal,* so the doctors had to deal with the addiction I now had to the drugs they'd been giving me. They abruptly cut off my morphine supply. Having to say goodbye to that drug was like saying goodbye to my best friend, but I gritted my teeth and waited for the welcome shot of Demerol to take effect.

It wasn't long before I'd practically swoon in ecstasy when the nurse entered the room with a syringe. As she swabbed my arm in preparation for the injection, the smell of alcohol started me salivating like Pavlov's dog.

When the nurses gave me Darvon, they'd have to split open the capsule and pour the powder onto my tongue because I couldn't swallow anything. Even if I somehow managed to choke down a bit of food or liquid, it immediately came back up.

The doctor simply assumed I'd lost my will to live, but later he found that hydrochloric acid and gastric juices had burned a hole in my stomach while I was in the coma. These acids had then washed back and dissolved the lower three inches of my esophagus, making it impossible for me to swallow.

After finally realizing I was starving to death, the doctor made an incision in my abdomen and inserted a 14-inch-long tube through the stomach wall. The nurses then poured nutritional liquid and vitamins directly into this gastrostomy tube, but it wasn't enough to compensate for the thousands of calories my body was burning every 24 hours. My 167 pounds of solid muscle rapidly melted away.

This hospital wasn't prepared to deal with a mess like me, and the severity of my condition pushed everyone to the limit. One weekend no one showed up to change the dressing on my badly burned right hand, and when a nurse finally removed the bandages on Monday morning, it looked like roadkill. When Dan came to visit me later that day, I could no longer swallow my self-pity.

"My hand looks like a piece of crap."

Dan immediately stood up, grabbed hold of my left hand and fixed me with his powerful stare. "Don't say that, Mickey. You're going to be okay. You're going to walk out of here alive and well, do you hear me?"

Dan considered it his sacred duty to continually drag me from wreckages. Even after the shadow of death had passed, he stayed close by to chase the vultures away from my bedside.

I used the word *vultures* to identify the dark spiritual forces skulking in the corners of my room. Birds of prey always hover near death, so Intensive Care was the perfect place for dark spirits trying to feast on the hopes of dying men. I'd never known about such things before the crash, but many lonely nights of imprisonment in that hospital sobered me to the reality of spiritual warfare.

Invisible vultures of fear, hopelessness, self-pity and despair would wait in the shadows until everyone was gone, then soar forth to perch silently on the end of my bed. They kept vigil during the darkest hours of the night, and I could even feel them hovering whenever certain people entered the room.

My journey to heaven had so sensitized me that I could almost smell people's attitudes. While some of my visitors wore a perfume of hope, others wore a stench of defeat. And it was the same with the doctors and nurses. Some kindly lifted me toward life while others let me slide toward death.

And then there were the candy stripers. These teenage volunteers didn't treat patients like gruesome statistics, but rather blessed us all with their innocent offerings of kindness and respect.

Each evening, a lovely sixteen-year-old wheeled her cart next to my bed and chirped, "Dinnertime!" Although I could smell the welcome fragrance of food, all I had to look forward to was a plastic bag filled with white glop.

As the candy striper hung the bag on the pole and attached my feeding tube, I counted the dreaded seconds until the cold ooze reached my stomach. While I lay there shivering and miserable, she'd flash me a radiant smile and say, "Don't worry, Mr. Robinson. It won't be long before I'll be bringing you a food tray." Such a simple thing to say, yet it was powerful enough to get me through those hopeless moments.

Even the smallest act of kindness became an essential part of my recovery. The first time Julie's mom asked if she could rub my legs, I was more than a little apprehensive. Yet when I felt the warmth of her hands, my heavily-bandaged legs responded to the life in her touch.

I started to cry, as it had been so long since someone had approached me without a needle or scalpel up their sleeve. It wasn't long before I began asking all my visitors to gently massage my stricken body.

Everyone had to wear gowns, masks and gloves, and some of them probably felt extremely uncomfortable with my hands-on request. But others saw it as an opportunity to help lessen my unending pain.

My brother was one of my most faithful caregivers. Every day after school, he walked or hitchhiked to the hospital. He would sit there hour after hour, gently squeezing my legs. He never gave up on me, and his commitment was one of the sparks that kindled life back into my broken body.

My skydiving buddy, Jerry, often drove one and a half hours to the hospital just to visit with me for a few minutes. Although one of the elite, Jerry wasn't ashamed to sit by the bed and literally squeeze life into my left hand. Without such human kindness, I would never have survived.

Every day I got stacks of encouraging letters, and sometimes the guys from the drop zone would come to the hospital and show me skydiving films. Although I loved their visits, I was no longer comfortable with their foul language and casual references to sex. When a well-meaning friend came by to give me a Playboy magazine, I tried my best to act polite, but he could tell I wasn't interested.

Cornering my sister in the hospital hallway later that afternoon, he asked, "What's with Mickey? Has he become religious or something?"

My sister looked at him in disbelief and said, "Mickey? You gotta be kidding!"

It was heaven that had changed me, but how could I explain that to them? I didn't understand it myself. Yet, I was now aware that certain things weakened my spirit, and the only thing standing between the grave and me was the strength of my spirit.

Dan understood that, and somehow he always showed up when I was at my weakest. Once I lingered in a coma for several days while members of my family sat by the bedside calling, "Mickey, wake up!" But I didn't respond.

Then Dan showed up at the hospital, and just as he stepped out of the elevator, I opened my eyes. Ever since the day Dan had pulled me toward himself in the sky while sky-diving, our spirits had been linked. That's why the dream I had one night was especially evil—like a telegram straight from hell.

In this dream, I was standing at the top of a deep, dark stairwell. Dan was standing next to me, pointing downward and whispering in my ear, "Go ahead, Mickey. What are you waiting for? Get it over with."

Even though fast asleep, I managed to grab the bed's steel bars with my left hand and start banging my head against them. After a nurse ran in and mercifully woke me, I lay there silently shivering in fear. Why would I dream that the person who'd saved my life was now pointing me toward death? Something was trying to inject me with despair.

No matter what went on in that hospital, I had to focus on staying alive. Since I couldn't sit up or move around in bed, it was impossible for me to see the other patients, but I could hear them. And there were days I felt like a priest having to listen to a relentless confession of human suffering.

Day after day they wheeled people in who were more dead than alive, like the man across from me whose name was Pat. He'd been working in a gas station during a robbery, and after the thief stole $30 from the cash register, he'd directed Pat to walk toward the back of the store. Then the thief unloaded a shotgun into his back and left him lying there, paralyzed from the waist down.

Pat was immobilized on a Stryker frame that flipped him upside down every few hours like a human pancake. Though he rarely spoke, once in awhile I'd hear him begging the nurses, "Can I have another LifeSaver?"

The man in the bed next to me was also a burn victim. He'd worked in an auto shop. One day when he wasn't looking, some practical joker put the end of an oxygen hose down his pants. When he innocently lit up a cigarette, the lower half of his body went up in flames.

Another patient had been in a bad car accident and broken practically every bone in his body. They covered him in a full plaster cast, and day after day he lay there immobilized in the shape of a big white X.

In addition to looking like a bunch of creatures from the Black Lagoon, we were all as helpless as newborns. I couldn't even go to the bathroom without asking the nurses for help. The first six weeks I had a catheter, and afterwards a bedpan. I hated that. I hated having to depend on another person to empty my bladder, quench my thirst, fill my stomach, relieve my pain and render me even the slightest bit of comfort.

Many times when I yelled for help, I'd hear a voice say, "Okay, okay, we're coming." But no one came. And when I looked out the door, I could see the nurses sitting there drinking coffee, smoking cigarettes and ignoring me. Maybe they thought I was delirious, or maybe they were just incredibly weary from having to deal with all the pain in ICU.

I was allowed to have a little transistor radio on the table by my bed, so I kept it turned down low to WIXY-1260. The number one song at that time was "Light My Fire," and needless to say, it was not one of my favorites. Neither was the one that started out with some lunatic screaming, "I am the god of hell fire!" Whenever that song played, I lay there in physical torment. The words and music scraped across my soul like fingernails, but I couldn't move to turn the radio off. I'd just have to lie there helplessly and suffer through until the next song.

When they'd play, "The Harper Valley PTA," a woman on the other side of the room would start screaming, "Yeah .. . that's me! I socked it to The Harper Valley PTA! That's me!" Then she'd start laughing like a maniac.

I put up with this for a few days, but then broke my silence and politely said, "Excuse me, ma'am. I'm 19 years old, and I'm in a lot of pain. Could you please keep it down?"

"Oh yeah, kid," she muttered. "Yeah, you're beautiful, kid." She'd quiet down for five minutes, and then start ranting and raving all over again. Perhaps she'd overdosed on drugs, or maybe she'd just lost her mind altogether.

This den of weirdness was my home for many weeks, and every day my faithful mother came for a visit. No matter how bad I looked or how many complications arose, she never for a moment thought I would die. Week after week she'd innocently ask the doctor, "Is he out of the woods yet?"

Only six months earlier she'd ended twenty-five years of marriage and gone to work as a waitress in order to make house payments. A mortally wounded son was the last thing she needed, but my mother didn't flinch. She bravely spent all her free time at my bedside, usually more concerned with my weight than with my mortality.

The first time Julie saw me conscious, she exercised incredible self-control. As I watched her come in the door and walk toward my bed, I thought she looked like a beautiful angel strolling through a corpse-strewn battlefield. But when she calmly leaned over to kiss me, I watched her eyes dart around my face, looking for an uncharred place to touch her lips to.

After courageously kissing me on the left side of my forehead, she flashed me a nervous little smile. But as I tried to respond to her, she instinctively pulled away. It was then I saw the mixture of fear, guilt and confusion in her eyes. She was totally blown away. And how could I blame her? Her handsome boyfriend no longer existed in this present state.

As Julie stared solemnly at my emaciated body, I said, "As soon as I can get out of this bed, I'm gonna start working out. You'll see! I'm gonna be in better shape than before—185 lbs. and stronger than ever."

"No! Don't do that, Mickey," Julie exclaimed. "I liked you just the way you were."

Although she didn't realize the irony of that remark, to me it came through loud and clear. I had been expecting her to share in my dreams for recovery, but she was only twenty years old. This was too much for her to handle.

After I passed the initial crisis, Julie's parents encouraged her to return to college. She had missed the first month of the term, so she must have been relieved to return to normal life and normal faces. Still, she faithfully continued to write me every day.

One afternoon while I was waiting for the mail, a stranger walked into the Intensive Care Unit wearing a suit and tie. He stood by the side of my bed and asked, "Would you mind if I prayed for you?"

No one had ever asked me that question, so I said, "Sure, why not?"

"Is it okay if I read some things from the Bible?"

"Yeah, go ahead."

He cracked open this huge black book and started to read, *"Surely He hath borne our griefs, and carried our sorrows. He was wounded for our trangressions, he was bruised for our iniquities . . . "*

I was only half listening, and didn't even understand what the words meant, but within a few seconds, a little earthquake started inside the pit of my stomach. It quickly rose up into my chest and I began to shake violently.

Ordinarily I didn't have the strength to move a muscle, but now I was shaking so hard that the chrome bars of the bed banged against the wall. As the earthquake reached my throat, I half expected to start vomiting uncontrollably. But instead I cried out, "I've gotta be some kinda priest or something! I've been reborn!"

The man with the Bible looked down at me in complete shock. He probably thought he was going to get sued for throwing me into a seizure, so he kept trying to calm me down.

"You're gonna be okay," he said over and over. "Just quiet down. You're gonna be alright." Then he quickly disappeared down the hall, and I never saw him again. That man probably ran out of the hospital and changed his name, even though he hadn't done anything wrong.

When he read those Scriptures out loud, something awoke inside of me and immediately wanted out. But how could a sentence from a religious book like the Bible have that kind of effect on me? I'd never even heard the word *reborn* before—what did it mean? I was too tired to think about all this, so I just pulled the blanket over my trembling body and fell into a deep sleep.

Chapter Fourteen

Walking with the Wounded

Early one morning, the ordinarily quiet Intensive Care Unit came alive with activity. White-clad nurses and orderlies dashed in and out of the darkened room, descending on patients like a flock of hungry gulls. "Wake up, Mr. Robinson," said one orderly as he wheeled a gurney next to my bed. "We're moving you to the first floor."

"Why?"

"We need to do some cleaning in here. Don't worry, you'll be well taken care of."

The man in the body cast had developed a staph infection, so they had to move everyone immediately in order to prevent further contagion. I almost welcomed the change until I discovered the first floor staff had no idea how to deal with a mess like me.

The nurses wouldn't allow me to stay in bed when they changed the sheets, but always insisted on lifting me out and plopping me into a wheelchair. Sitting there slumped over like a sack of flour, I honestly began to hate the smell of clean sheets. One day I was so weak that I begged the nurses, "Please don't move me. I can't . . . "

"Doctor's orders, Mr. Robinson! It'll only take a minute."

They rang for an orderly, but when he didn't show up, the nurses decided to move me themselves. With the bottom sheet acting as a sling, I was lifted off the bed and maneuvered toward the wheelchair. But just as they were about to put me down, one nurse lost her grip and dropped me to the floor.

Lying there unconscious, with several bones protruding from my ninety-pound body, I must have looked like the carcass of a Thanksgiving turkey. I don't know how long I was unconscious, but when I woke up I was back in bed surrounded by smiling nurses asking, "Can we get you anything, Mr. Robinson? Are you comfortable now, Mr. Robinson?"

The first floor was scary. The unfamiliar routine filled me with dread, and each evening after my family went home, I became paralyzed with fear. What if something would happen to me during the night? What if there would be an emergency and no one would be around?

At one point during those oppressive weeks, some old friends came to visit. Clint had been a quarterback on my football team, and Karen was our local high school beauty who later became runner-up for Miss America.

"How ya doin', Mickey?" said Clint, grabbing my left hand and holding it for a few seconds. I could see his eyes cloud over with pity as he said, "Are they treating you okay?"

I'd known Clint and Karen since grade school. But as I stared up at their perfect faces, I suddenly felt a million miles away. And as they talked on about mutual friends, my brain began cycling through its daily list of unanswerable questions: *How come this had to happen? Why couldn't I have just broken my leg? Why do I have to be so messed up?*

Then I began to vomit uncontrollably. As a nurse came running in, Clint and Karen backed against the wall and politely averted their eyes. After standing there for what seemed like an eternity, they finally muttered an embarrassed goodbye and disappeared down the hall. If I hadn't been retching my guts out, I would've felt humiliated. But I was too sick to care.

Life on the first floor was bleak, and I continued to spiral downward—until one morning when I opened my eyes and beheld the smiling face of a savior.

"Rise and shine, young man!" said a middle-aged woman wearing funky glasses and a nurse's cap. "I'm Mrs. Kruchek and today we're moving you to Two West so I can take care of you. I think you need some taking care of, honey."

But as the orderlies started to lift me onto the gurney, her eyes widened with horror.

"Oh my Lord, what happened here?" she asked, while staring at my feet.

It looked like someone had chopped off my heels with an axe. The constant pressure from lying in one position day after day had cut off circulation to my capillaries, and as a result, the flesh on my heels had begun to disintegrate.

Mrs. Kruchek immediately put the sheet back over my legs and disappeared into the hall. Within a few minutes, I could hear pieces of her conversation with the ICU head nurse.

"There's no excuse . . . I've never seen such bedsores . . . this should never have happened!"

Listening to the no-nonsense tone of her voice, I breathed a sigh of relief. Mrs. Kruchek was going to fight for me. She was actually the patron saint of all who lived on Two West, the ward where they deposited the horribly injured and the nearly dead. This incredible woman had faith enough for even the most hopeless cases, and her loving presence soon changed the direction of my body's condition.

But the first time she wheeled me toward the whirlpool, I cringed at the thought of anything touching my skin. As an orderly lifted me in, Mrs. Kruchek said, "You've got to trust me on this one, honey. It's going to make you feel better."

When they dumped in a whole box of diaper soap, I closed my eyes and gritted my teeth in anticipation of the pain. Instead I discovered the merciful healing of hot water, and for the first time in several months, I felt no pain.

The water turned blood red as pieces of dead tissue sloughed off my body and floated to the surface. But when they lifted me out and the air hit my naked flesh, I fainted dead away. As the orderly wheeled me onto the elevator, I woke up and asked, "How soon can I go back there?"

I flourished in Mrs. Kruchek's care, and by December I was allowed to make my first attempt at standing. As the physical therapist rolled my wheelchair onto a wooden platform between two parallel bars, he looked at me intently and said, "You think you're ready for this, Mickey?"

"Just get me out of this chair and I'll show you how ready I am."

He took two strips of Velcro with loops of elastic sewn on. He belted one under each of my knees. After pulling the pieces of elastic down, he looped them around my slippers to keep my feet from dropping whenever I took a step. Next, he cinched a canvas strap around my waist.

With this apparatus, the therapist lifted me out of the wheelchair and stood my shrunken 100-lb body between the parallel bars. He was actually supporting my weight by holding fast to the waist strap, but it felt enough like standing to exhilarate me.

Gripping one bar with my left arm, I carefully dragged my right leg a few inches forward, then my left. Summoning all my strength, I managed another half step before collapsing backwards into the wheelchair with an exhausted shout of triumph.

Then I felt something tickling my legs. Looking down, I discovered that all my patchwork plastic surgery had cracked open. Rivulets of blood were streaming down my legs and filling my slippers, but I was too tired to care. I felt as if I'd just skied down ten mountains, and couldn't even stay awake long enough to make it back to my room.

I slept for 24 hours, and when I finally woke up, I immediately wanted to get back on my feet. Although the doctors began to schedule appointments for physical therapy and the whirlpool, they were reluctant to give me any prognosis.

I desperately wanted to find out how I was doing, so when a technician tested my legs with electrodes, I carefully watched his face for a reaction. He seemed hopeful about the reflexes on my right leg, but when he tested the left, his face went blank. Though he didn't say a word, his silence told me the nerves in my left leg were dead.

It wasn't long before I began to hear rumors about being transferred to a rehabilitation hospital. I had now been at Southwest General for more than four months.

"Highland View can do a lot more for you than we can, honey," explained Mrs. Kruchek. "They have incredible equipment. I think they even have a Hubbard tank." Although I had no idea what a Hubbard tank was, I started to imagine Highland View as a virtual Disneyland for people like me.

"Did you know they're going to let you go home for a few hours during the transfer?" asked Mrs. Kruchek enthusiastically. "I'll bet you can't wait to see this place in a rear-view mirror!"

She was right. I was counting the days until my discharge, but I didn't want to leave the same way I came in.

Day after day in physical therapy, I fixated on being able to walk through my own front door. It seemed I had a good chance of reaching that goal until, just one night before the transfer, something unexpected happened.

I had almost fallen asleep when an agonizing itch started in my ankles and moved quickly up my legs. Within seconds, I felt like I'd just rolled in poison ivy and swallowed a gallon of red ants. My body was in so much internal and external torment, I could barely breathe. For some reason, unbeknownst to me, an uncontrollable itching spread through me, covering my entire body.

In reaction to the incredible stress, my stomach produced enough acid to melt the inflated rubber stopper on my gastrostomy tube. As if in some weird horror movie, the stopper suddenly blew off and released a spewing fountain of stomach acid. While one nurse frantically worked to close the opening, several others scurried around trying to wash the burning liquid off my skin.

Needless to say, I did not walk out of that hospital in triumph. As they slid my stretcher into an ambulance the next day, I no longer cared about walking. But nothing could quell the excitement my brother and my mom felt about my homecoming. They sat next to me in the back of the ambulance, chattering like two little kids whose father was returning home from the war.

"We're almost there, Mickey. Now we're passing the corner of Snow and Pearl, and there's the Convenience Mart on the left. We had a storm last night, so the neighborhood looks all clean and white. Everyone's waiting for you."

When the paramedics slid my stretcher from the ambulance and carried me up the walkway, I could see living room curtains moving in all the nearby houses. The whole neighborhood was watching my slow and silent grand entrance.

It was January 20, 1969, and after being institutionalized for five months I'd almost forgotten there was life beyond those hospital walls. But when they carried me across the threshold, our plain little house looked more beautiful than Buckingham Palace. Peering into the living room, I could see the faces of family and friends as they proudly gathered around a dried-up little Christmas tree. My mom had left it standing just for me, and as I stared at the flickering lights, I began to cry.

I don't remember much of what people said or did that night. All I remember is love and a sense of belonging I hadn't felt since I experienced heaven. As my sister placed a stick of incense in my left hand, she held up the new Jimi Hendrix album and proudly said, "Look what I bought you for Christmas!" With acid rock pounding, incense burning and everyone trying to talk all at once, my sister leaned over, gently kissed me on the cheek and whispered, "Welcome home, big brother."

Lying there, basking in all the attention, I almost forgot how sick I was. When I had to go to the bathroom, one of my friends volunteered to carry me, but attempting to sit on the toilet just made me pass out. When I woke up on the bathroom floor a few seconds later, my friend was cradling my head.

"You shouldn't have come home, Mickey," he said sadly. "You're too sick."

The next day an ambulance carried me to my new home at Highland View, a 400-bed hospital designed for double amputees, quadriplegics, people with head injuries—and worse. Some patients would stay for many months, while others would linger forever.

They let my mother accompany me into the examining room that first day. I hadn't taken any medication, so when the nurse started to remove my bandages I nearly went through the roof. I was in so much pain I failed to notice the look on my mother's face.

She'd never seen my unbandaged body before, and I could vaguely hear her mumbling, *Holy Mary, Mother of God,* as she quickly escalated toward hysteria. Ultimately, the nurses had to remove her from the room to calm her down.

The doctor wanted to immediately schedule me for skin grafts, so I was permanently assigned to the surgical ward. But when the nurse wheeled me in to meet my three paralyzed roommates, I looked around and thought, "I hope these guys are livelier than they look."

Bob was a law student who'd been paralyzed from the neck down in a car accident. Roy was an Appalachian redneck who'd been paralyzed from the waist down as a result of a gunshot wound. Larry was a young black man who'd become quadriplegic after breaking his neck in a car accident.

Only the strangest twist of fate could have made roommates of a redneck, a black man, a law student and a skydiver. Although the four of us had nothing in common, we were stuck in our broken bodies and stuck with each other.

Before my accident, I never even knew places like Highland View existed. I was living with people who couldn't walk, and some who could barely move, yet they taught me that human existence doesn't begin and end with the body. Life goes on, with or without your legs.

My paralyzed roommates were as alive as anyone I'd ever met. They still laughed, they still dreamed, and their blood pressure still soared whenever a pretty girl walked into the room. Although they tried to be on their best behavior when my sister came to visit, her mere presence sent sparks flying. After she left one day, Bob said, "Hey, Mickey, your sister's so good looking!"

"Yeah, I guess so."

"Ya know what I'm going to do? Next time she comes, I'm going to have her come over and talk to me. Then when she's real close, I'll have a spasm so my arm can slide onto her leg. Whaddya think?"

"I think you're a weirdo, Bob."

"Yeah, well, you're one of us now, Robinson. What're you going to say when people stare at you? You've got to think of something good to say."

"I'll just tell 'em I made an ash of myself."

My roommates laughed so hard, they almost rolled off their Stryker frames. They loved to have fun, and they loved it when people came to visit. Patients need life from outside as much as plants need sunlight, and since I was blessed with many visitors, I gladly shared the wealth with my roommates. They quickly adopted my friends and family, and of course, they knew all about Julie, who was still the most important part of my plans for the future.

She visited often, her parents came, she wrote me, and we kept communicating. I think I clung to Julie and to skydiving in an attempt to resurrect what I had lost in the accident.

Late one night, a nurse came in and said, "There's a person-to-person call for you, Mickey." As I got into my wheelchair and headed for the door, Bob said, "Make it convincing, lover boy!"

I lived for phone calls from Julie, but I tried not to sound anxious as I picked up the receiver at the pay phone down the hall.

"Hi . . . you at home?"

"No, I'm still at school. I just wanted to talk to you."

"What's goin' on?"

There was dead silence for a few seconds before a voice I barely recognized said, "I've been thinking about us, Mickey. I don't think I can be with you anymore."

My heart was in my mouth as I tried to form words.

"Don't say that! We're gonna get married, and then spend the rest of our lives together. I'm gonna be okay, Julie! Don't just . . . "

"I've thought about this for a long time, Mickey. It's what I have to do. I'm sorry. I can't be with you anymore. I'm sorry."

When I heard the click of the receiver, something switched off inside me. Suddenly, it didn't matter whether I was alive or dead, and I barely remembered to breathe as I wheeled back down the hall. Although I purposely kept my head down as I quietly entered the room, Larry immediately asked, "What'd she say? Is she coming up this weekend?"

"Can she bring a friend?" asked Bob. "Does she have any friends who like guys that are tall, dark and paralyzed?"

But the joking stopped when they realized something was wrong. I didn't say a word as I crawled into bed, turned my face to the wall and stuffed a pillow in my mouth to stifle the sobs. I wanted to run and keep on running until I fell off the edge of the earth, but I couldn't. I had to just lay there and feel the pain.

I wept all through the night, but right before dawn Larry woke up and heard my muffled sobs. Although the blanket was over my head, I could hear someone talking to me in a strangely tender voice.

"Don't you worry, Mickey. They're gonna fix you up," he whispered from across the room. "You're gonna get out of here and be back on the street, just you wait and see. You're gonna be cool again."

All of a sudden, I thought Larry was right beside my bed. Exhausted from weeping, I turned and looked across the room, but he hadn't moved. He couldn't move, yet he seemed closer than a whisper and his words felt like a cool hand on my burning forehead. I never told Larry what his words meant to me, but just three weeks later I was able to return the kindness.

At three o'clock in the morning, I awoke to the terrible sound of crashing metal. As I sat up in bed and looked around the darkened room, I saw that the metal weights suspended by Larry's bed had fallen to the floor. Following his spinal fusion, the doctors had drilled holes on either side of Larry's skull and placed weighted metal tongs inside the holes to hold his neck in place. For some reason, those tongs had slipped out and sent 35 pounds of metal slamming to the floor.

Larry's head was now totally unprotected, and if he'd had a spasm or jerked even slightly, his head could have rolled off the Stryker frame and severed his spinal cord. When I shook myself awake enough to realize what had happened, I immediately rang for the nurse.

Crawling out of bed, I dragged myself across the room and carefully positioned my bandaged hands on either side of Larry's face. I was holding his life in my hands at that moment, and as I stood there looking down at him, overwhelming love began to pour through me.

As nurses and orderlies ran into the room, Larry looked up at me like a frightened little boy and whispered, "Mickey?"

"Yeah, Larry, I'm here. Don't worry, I won't let you go."

After the crisis was over, I tried to go back to sleep, but I couldn't. Love was still pouring through me, but it wasn't the love I'd felt for Julie. It went beyond feelings, and even beyond compassion. It was the love of God, and reaching out to Larry had just caused it to overflow.

A few weeks later, I was sitting on the bed trying to practice writing with my left hand.

"Mickey, there's somebody here for you," Bob said.

I looked up to see my father standing in the doorway. I was too stunned to say anything as he walked slowly and cautiously over to my bed, but I remember thinking how old he looked.

"Hello, son," he said softly. "How're you feeling?" Before I could answer, he nervously cleared his throat, mumbled "Just a minute," and then disappeared into the hall.

"Well, I guess he hasn't changed," I said to my curious roommates. "I don't see my dad for a year, and he still can't talk to me."

When he came back a few minutes later, I could tell he'd been crying. I'd never seen my father cry except when his mother died, so the uncharacteristic display of emotion made me uneasy. I tried to lighten things up by making small talk, but it was no use. My usually flippant and sarcastic father remained strangely silent.

He was a broken man. After losing his wife and his job just six months before my accident, he'd accepted a much lower paying position in order to keep on working. My father was living alone in a little apartment on the West Side, which was a far cry from our nice neighborhood in Independence.

I usually had to be on guard against his sharp tongue, but this time I didn't feel the need to protect myself. He behaved like a total gentleman as he lingered by my bedside. Yet, I began to sense my father's overwhelming grief over my devastating condition.

The sight of me was too much for him, but it wasn't just affecting him emotionally. My physical condition was challenging everything he believed about human justice. In his simple philosophy, the innocent were rewarded and the guilty punished. There was just no way he could fit my suffering into his tidy calculation.

"I don't get it, Mickey," he said finally. "I'm old and I drink too much. I've made a mess of everything, but you're just a young man! How could this happen to you?"

"I don't know, Dad," I answered honestly. "Maybe life isn't as simple as you think. Maybe people don't always get what they deserve."

He couldn't understand what I was saying yet, as he stood there looking confused, I suddenly realized he cared about me. And for the first time in many years I wanted to care about him.

"Dad," I whispered tearfully. "Why did it have to be like this?" With his head bowed in shame and his mask of sarcasm totally removed, I saw a man I'd never seen before.

Because he'd shut me out so early on, I'd never really felt like his son. But as I wept for our broken relationship, a genuine love for my father came flooding in. Although still a stranger in many ways, my dad was no longer an enemy. When we said goodbye that day, I sensed an unspoken peace between us, and that peace was to continue until the day he died.

Chapter Fifteen

No Turning Back

After seven months of hospitalization and rehabilitation, I was beginning to show signs of real improvement. Mobility meant freedom, and day-by-day I was reclaiming the little freedoms I'd once taken for granted. After all those months of lying in bed staring at the ceiling, I was incredibly thankful just to be able to sit by a window and look outside.

Although I was still a full-time patient, I had learned to speed up and down the hallways in my trusty wheelchair, eat in the cafeteria, and basically hang out with the 1,001 beings who called Highland View *home*. I was no longer merely a survivor but had become an active participant in my own recovery.

The doctors were constantly figuring out new ways to put Mickey back together again, and at this point they decided to try and stretch out my scarred esophagus. After making me drink something that tasted like STP Oil Treatment, the doctor had me lie down on a table with my head over the edge.

As he slid a bronchoscope down my throat, I gripped the table with my left hand and thought: *Now I know what it feels like to be a sword swallower.* When he stepped back to let a bunch of medical students look down my throat, I felt just like a frog in biology class. But the worst was yet to come.

My scarred esophagus was less than one sixteenth of an inch wide, so as the doctor pulled a bullet-shaped piece of silver through the opening, I crossed my eyes in pain. It felt as if Knut Rockne was dragging a football through my insides.

This metal *bullet* had to be dragged through my esophagus twice a week for several months, so the doctor left me with a green string hanging out of my nose and some parting words of encouragement.

"I can't promise anything, Mickey," he said soberly. "With the extent of your injuries, I don't know if your esophagus will ever function normally. I suspect you'll have to have this procedure repeated twice a year for the rest of your life."

I couldn't understand how this medieval string torture could help me swallow, but it did, and it wasn't long before I was able to eat five bowls of soup and mashed potatoes at one meal. To a man who hadn't eaten in seven months, it tasted better than steak and lobster.

Recovery became my full-time job, and I threw myself into it with characteristic passion. Luckily, the therapists at Highland View were equally passionate about bringing me back to life. They didn't pamper me because they knew that making me walk was a whole lot more important than making me comfortable.

The doctors were continually grafting pieces of skin onto my right hand and neck, but due to all the scar tissue I couldn't lift my right arm more than six inches from my side. And because of the tightened skin grafts on my neck, I wasn't even able to turn my head from side to side.

This would have been frustrating for anyone, but as an athlete I was doubly frustrated. However, I was used to warring against my physical limitations, so I began to use that same fierceness to restore the mobility I'd lost.

The process of therapy seemed much too slow. So when no one was looking, I would painfully twist my arm back and forth until one day I heard a loud snap and I regained some freedom of movement! After doing the same thing with my neck, I was able to regain some of the flexibility I'd lost in it.

But I still had bilateral foot drop and extensive nerve damage in my left leg. The day I was fitted with a leg brace, the doctor said, "You'd better get used to wearing this,

Mickey, because you're going to be wearing it the rest of your life."

I could barely tolerate those words, and without thinking, I stood up and said, "No way. I'm not leaving this hospital wearing a brace." Those words burst out of me in a torrent of faith that had nothing to do with positive thinking. This faith was a gift from heaven, and it was much more powerful than any physical limitation or medical opinion.

From that day on, I made it a point to start speaking *life* to my leg. I would lie in bed every night, put my hand on it and whisper, "Life . . . blood . . . strength . . . go into this leg." I couldn't go to physical therapy on surgery days, so I stayed in my room and did a leg workout using small sandbags and weights. I never abandoned this routine, even though the muscles reaching from my kneecap to my foot were totally unresponsive.

One day, while performing this ritual in my room, the nerves in my left leg suddenly sprang to life. As I watched my foot move for the first time since the accident, I yelled out to my roommates, "Did you see that?"

"See what?" said Bob, half asleep and totally disinterested.

"My foot moved! My leg's gonna be okay!" I enthusiastically pressed the buzzer and called every nurse within earshot. They were all amazed, and when the doctor arrived, he didn't even try to offer an explanation.

He just grabbed my wheelchair and said, "Let's go and shock some people." Rolling me in and out of practically every clinic in that hospital, my doctor would casually say, "I'd like to show you a new procedure we developed in surgery today."

Then he would gently pull on the green string hanging out of my nose, which was my cue to immediately kick my left leg up in the air. The hoots of laughter that followed were music to my ears. The whole hospital was celebrating one sweet moment of triumph in the midst of unbelievable odds.

Nothing seemed impossible because of my heaven-sent determination to live. Yet in order to hold onto that determination, I had to ignore comments such as, "It's so sad. You're such a young man." I couldn't afford to listen to such misguided expressions of mercy. I was too busy getting well to feel sorry for myself.

Each and every morning I went to either physical therapy or the infamous Hubbard tank. An orderly would hoist my stretcher up on a chain and then submerge me slowly into the stainless steel tank shaped like a cross. As the hot water bubbled and heaved against my body, one therapist worked on my legs while another exercised my right arm.

In the afternoons I went to occupational therapy (OT), which was the hardest part of the day for me. Although they taught me useful things like how to tie my shoes or how to button my shirt with one hand, I hated OT. It always made me feel as if I had to settle for less.

"Losing a hand is a very crippling injury," explained one therapist. "In many ways, it's easier to lose your leg." Although they were just trying to be realistic, I sometimes felt the therapists were trying to steal my thunder. Their job was to prepare me for my role as a handicapped person, but sewing wallets wasn't going to be part of my future. I was going to live, and live big. No amount of common sense could take that away from me.

Some patients just sat around and watched TV, but I didn't have time for that. I used every spare moment to explore the highways and byways of Highland View, and it wasn't long before I discovered the Art Studio. Mickey McGraw, a paraplegic who whipped around in her wheelchair, smiling and singing and breathing life into everyone she met, ran it.

Although I'd always been a natural artist, I didn't know what to expect once I lost the use of my right hand. But when I explained my predicament to Mickey McGraw, she just said, "You don't know what you can do until you try. Sometimes being crippled can unleash creativity, so grab a piece of paper."

She was right. I immediately began drawing as well with my left hand as I had with my right. Although I still couldn't sign my name legibly, sailboats and palm trees appeared magically onto the paper. I was like a kid let loose with a billion crayons, and the pictures just flowed out of me non-stop.

I couldn't wait for late afternoons when I'd park myself in the little studio to sketch and listen to music. With "Pinball Wizard" booming out of the stereo, I spent hours drawing scenes of South Sea Islands and snow-covered mountains. My heart soared beyond those hospital walls, and with each stroke of the pen I was dreaming up adventures for my exciting future.

I still yearned to make spiritual connection here on earth, but I didn't know how. I didn't know there was any way to approach God except through the Catholic church, and since the Bible hadn't been part of my religious upbringing, I never considered reading it.

On Ash Wednesday, I decided to attend the little Catholic mass held at Highland View. Palm fronds are traditionally burned on the Sunday before Lent, and then on Ash Wednesday the priest crosses foreheads with ashes to signify, *From dust we came, and to dust we will return.*

Wanting desperately to connect with something, I wheeled up to the altar and asked the priest to make the sign of the cross on my forehead. I was a little taken aback when he just smiled pleasantly, put his hand on my shoulder and said, "I think those rituals are sort of masochistic. You don't really need that."

I believe the young priest was politely trying to point me beyond religious ritual, but his words just left me feeling confused. Wasn't communion with God dependent on ritual? How could I make spiritual connection without a priest? As I left that mass feeling frustrated and dismayed, the same question kept haunting me: *Where on earth could I find the love I'd felt in heaven?*

Since I was feeling better physically, I began to yearn for life outside Highland View. When I learned that some patients had gotten permission to spend eight hours with their families, I started bugging the doctors for a day pass. Life before the crash had taken on almost mythological significance, so I naturally planned to head back to the scene of my greatest triumph—the sky. I really wanted to take a plane ride from the airport where I'd made my first jump, but I kept this little plan a secret from everyone but my roommates.

"Ride in an airplane?" said Larry incredulously. "Are you crazy? After what you've been through, you want to get back in an airplane?"

"Yeah, why not?" I asked matter-of-factly.

"You know what I like about you, Mickey?" laughed Bob. "You've got more guts than sense!"

A few days later, a friend came to pick me up for my first little excursion. Just riding to the airport was exciting, and when I stepped out and saw all my old friends, the horrors of the past eight months seemed to vanish.

Everyone was so glad to see that I was alive, they didn't even care what I looked like. Although Dale enthusiastically agreed to let me ride in his Cessna 180 with two other skydivers, he refused to let me wear a parachute.

"No way, Mickey," he said with a knowing grin. "You'd probably jump out when I opened the door, and then I'd have to scrape you off the ground with a spatula. Do me a favor? Wait until you're a little stronger, okay?"

Bracing myself for takeoff, I half expected to feel a twinge of fear. But as we picked up speed and left the ground, I felt totally calm. It was as if life had stopped at the exact moment of impact eight months ago and I was simply taking up where I'd left off. The accident hadn't stolen my desire, and I was sure it wouldn't be long before I was back in the sky again.

Just a few weeks later, I wrangled another day pass to attend the wedding of two dear friends. I'd long fantasized about surprising Frank and Lucia on their big day, and at the very last moment the doctors gave me permission. Although I had virtually nothing to wear, one of the nurses miraculously found me a blue suit that had either belonged to a very tall child or a very thin adult. After getting dressed, I summoned my courage, took a deep breath and stepped up to the mirror.

Although the walls of physical therapy were covered with mirrors, I'd somehow managed to avoid looking at myself. I remembered what Mickey Robinson looked like, and that face in the mirror wasn't his. Although I'd averted my eyes for many months, today I was feeling bold. And curious.

I stood there for several minutes, gazing steadily at the 110-pound man in the mirror. One half of his melted face was stained with silver nitrate, while the other half was a pale, lifeless gray. His burned scalp and frazzled hair resembled a fright wig, and there was a small piece of green string taped to the side of his nose. With a blackened front tooth and a bandage on his right hand, this emaciated man looked like he was getting ready to march in the Veteran's Day parade.

But I didn't see it that way. Looking intently at my disfigured reflection, I simply thought, *Wow, I'm looking so much better!* In fact, I couldn't wait to walk into that wedding. I was sure everyone would be blown away by the progress I'd made.

A friend drove me to the church but, by the time we walked in, the wedding was already in progress. Silently taking a seat in the back row, I immediately felt pain shoot through my skin-and-bones backside. I could barely sit on the hard wooden pew, but luckily the ceremony was almost over. Within a few minutes, the wedding party moved slowly back down the aisle.

While Frank was coming down the aisle, he spotted me and stopped dead in his tracks. As the rest of the wedding party walked into him, he suddenly let go of his new bride and ran over to shake my hand.

"Oh, man," he said joyfully. "I can't believe you're here! Lucia, look who made it to our wedding!"

She came over and gave me a little hug, but I could tell she was afraid I might fall apart if she squeezed too hard.

"Thanks for coming, Mickey," said Lucia kindly. "We didn't think you'd be with us today."

"I wanted to come and give you this," I said, handing them the drawing of a mountain lake I'd been working on for several weeks. I'd carefully etched Frank and Lucia's initials into the grain of a rock, and then had the drawing matted and framed for a wedding present.

Frank stared at it for a few seconds before noticing my signature on the bottom. "You drew this, Mickey?" he asked incredulously. "I can't believe you drew this left-handed!"

"Pretty cool, huh? You never know what you can do until you try."

As people continued to walk up and congratulate Frank and Lucia, they took one look at me and fumbled for words.

"Mickey! Wow! You're looking . . . better!"

"They let you out of the hospital already?"

"Are the doctors going to do plastic surgery on your face?"

People tried their best to be polite, but it was no use. They were here to have fun, and my presence made them think about things they didn't want to think about. All conversations were deliberately brief, and I ended up feeling very much alone.

As it turned out, Julie was Lucia's maid of honor. But I decided not to say hello to her, as the wound was still too fresh. However, as I was glancing around the room, we somehow made eye contact and Julie started walking toward me. Seeing her dressed for a wedding unnerved me, and as she got closer, I felt my face get hot.

Whisking by as if I was a casual acquaintance, Julie lowered her eyes and said, "You look really good." Then, after giving me a frozen kiss on the cheek, she quickly disappeared into the crowd.

Standing there in a room full of old friends, I suddenly realized I was looking at a life that didn't exist anymore. I decided it was time to go back to Highland View, but as I quietly headed for the door, I passed an underclassman from my old high school. He stared at me as if he'd just seen a ghost, and then followed me out to the parking lot. Although I knew who he was, I pretended not to recognize him.

"Mickey?" he called in disbelief. "Mickey Robinson? Wow, what happened to you? You really got messed up!" I didn't answer him, even though it was a perfect opportunity to use my famous line about making an ash of myself. I just didn't feel like being funny.

On the ride back to the hospital, I let myself feel the excruciating pain of loss. I no longer looked good, my athletic image had been shattered, and the right girl had walked out on me.

All that once mattered had been taken away. The old Mickey Robinson was dead. He'd died in that plane crash, and when I realized he wasn't coming back, I determined to meet the man who would take his place.

Chapter Sixteen

Re-entry

"We're gonna miss you, man," said Larry as I emptied the drawer of my bedside table into a small box. It was June 28, 1969, and I was being discharged from Highland View. Although dozens of surgical procedures still lay ahead of me, it was no longer necessary for me to be an inpatient. The long-awaited day had finally come, and I was going home!

"So what're you planning to do out there, hotshot?" asked Bob.

"I don't know," I answered honestly. "Probably get back into skydiving."

"Yeah, that's what I figured," he said laughingly. "But do yourself a favor, Mickey. Next time wear an asbestos jump-suit."

We stuck to small talk because saying goodbye would have taken us to a place we didn't want to go. I knew Bob and Larry would probably be spending the rest of their lives inside an institution, but they weren't jealous of me. My roommates were genuinely happy that one of us was finally getting to go home.

"I never thought you'd be leaving this place," admitted the nurse's aide who was helping me get my stuff together. "I wouldn't have given two cents for you when they rolled you in last January."

"Yeah, he was a mess," said Bob. "But now look at him. The kid could make a fortune selling fire insurance."

We all joked around until it was time to go, and then I abruptly stood to my feet and headed for the door. As far as I was concerned, walking out of that room ended my life as a patient. Although I was still facing years of complex procedures, I was mentally and emotionally done with sickness. Without a wheelchair, leg brace or support of any kind, I walked out of that hospital and declared myself a free man!

As soon as I got home, I wanted to call all my friends and tell them to come over, but there was no one left to call. College, marriage and Vietnam had scattered most of my classmates, and those who were still around had disappeared into a whole new culture. My hometown had become a bizarre world of white bell-bottoms, earth shoes, long hair and love beads. No longer knowing how to dress or even how to behave, I was left feeling like Ryp Van Robinson.

It didn't take long to discover that most people were too busy to hang out with a mangled twenty-year-old who couldn't even drive a car. Since I couldn't get by on charm or good looks anymore, I had to get busy finding out what kind of life I could salvage from the wreckage.

My brother-in-law kindly came by a few times to take me for rides, and one day we headed for McDonald's to try out their new 49-cent Big Mac. Everything was fine until a piece of hamburger lodged firmly in my scarred esophagus, and then I proceeded to gag and heave and turn blue until the food came flying out of my mouth into the parking lot. As I breathed a sigh of relief, he just stared at me in horror and said, "Oh, man, what a drag!" Needless to say, he never took me out for lunch again.

Just a week later, three old football friends stopped by my mother's house. Clint was the only one who'd ever visited me in the hospital, and he seemed genuinely impressed by the progress I'd made.

"You're looking better, Mickey. And it's good to see you're not throwing up anymore!"

"Yeah," I said with a laugh. "That was pretty gross, huh?"

I hadn't seen Jim since before the accident, and he solemnly stared at me as if I was a corpse on the highway. After several minutes, I finally looked him in the eye and said, "It's okay, Jim. My face is kind of tweaked, but I'm still the same Mickey."

He looked embarrassed, so I tried to lighten things up by pointing to the patches of skin covering my face and exclaiming, "I may look weird, but how many people do you know with a genuine paisley complexion?"

Jim laughed out loud, but the other two just forced a polite chuckle. Clint quickly changed the subject and said, "So what're you planning to do now, Mickey?"

I didn't know what to tell him, so I just answered, "Skydiving. I want to get back into free fall."

As the guys flashed each other knowing looks, an uncomfortable silence settled in the room. Finally Clint stood up and said, "I'm glad you're doing well, Mickey. We'll be seeing you around, okay?"

As I watched them pull out of the driveway, I knew they weren't coming back, but I refused to let it bother me. I still had skydiving. I still belonged somewhere.

One beautiful July afternoon, my brother and I had a plan. It was time for me to jump again, in a rather odd celebration of life! We put our parachutes in the car and invited my mother to drive over to the Cleveland School of Sport Parachuting with us. There was a pure blue sky and absolutely no wind, but as I got out of the car and walked across the runway, I felt weirdly disconnected.

There was no way of knowing how my 115-pound body would handle free fall, and I kept imagining myself getting caught in the jet stream and parasailing to Peru. I was still entertaining these anxious thoughts when I heard Dan's unmistakable voice say, "Ready to go, hotshot?"

"Sure," I said, putting a lid on my imagination while smiling broadly at my old friend. "I've been ready for a long time."

I jumped out at 12,500 feet, followed by my brother and then Dan. After all the stuffy hospital rooms and stinking bandages, I gratefully gulped the cool air I hadn't tasted for so long. The day was absolutely perfect, and when the three of us finally linked together and joined hands, I looked into their grinning faces and waited for the old rush to return.

But nothing happened.

Those few seconds of free fall had always been the purest experience of my life, but this time they seemed pale compared to the brilliance of eternity. Free fall was still amazing, but it was no longer the ultimate. I realized I wasn't addicted to skydiving anymore, because I knew there was something deeper and truer than the sky.

When I got back on the ground, a bunch of my old skydiving buddies came running up to congratulate me. Although I went through the motions of being really excited, something was missing. I was afraid Dan might notice my lack of enthusiasm, but when our eyes met, I could tell he was excited enough for both of us.

About a week later, I went back into Highland View for an operation to close up the hole in my stomach. Recuperating from that surgery was a lot more painful than I'd ever imagined, but I no longer wanted to be treated like a patient, so I downplayed the discomfort.

Then, in September, I began an endless round of reconstructive surgeries at Cleveland's University Hospital. Since I was constantly in and out of the operating room, surgery became my full-time job. I would check into the hospital, return home for a few weeks of recuperation, and then go right back in for another round.

While at home, I spent most of my time reading everything I could get my hands on. Desperate to find a link between the love of heaven and life on earth, I embarked on a ferocious quest for truth. Besides studying *Psychology Today* magazines and something called *PsychoCybernetics*, I began working my way through stacks of books by Baba Ram Dass, Paramahansa Yogananda, Lobsang Rampa and Hermann Hesse.

I knew the Beatles were beating a path toward India, so I started checking out some of the Eastern religions. Although a few were intellectually stimulating, I ultimately found them to be vague and unreal. Their mystical messages would glisten in my mind for a few days but then quickly fade like a cosmic mirage.

One day, while watching a television interview with Maharishi Mahesh Yogi, I heard him say, "This is that . . . and that is this . . . and all this is that, too."

"Oh, yeah, great," I said to my brother with a quizzical look on my face. "What the heck did that mean?"

"I think that means you should change the channel," he said matter-of-factly. We just couldn't get behind a little man with a big beard who sat around quoting fortune cookies.

I'd read in the newspaper about a guy who was teaching some kind of mind control, so I drove over to his house one day and sat in the living room with all the other truth seekers. When the teacher walked in and sat on the floor, we all gathered around to hear him describe his latest out-of-body experience.

"I was on the verge of another dimension," he said breathlessly with a gleam in his eye. "The next time it happens, I'm not holding back. The next time, I'm going for it."

While everyone gazed at him with dreamy-eyed intensity, I found myself thinking: *This guy's been watching too much Star Trek.* When he later asked me to share my experience, I talked a little about the crash and my time in the hospital, but I never mentioned heaven. I didn't want these people comparing it to some kind of celestial picnic.

After awhile, the teacher made us close our eyes while he played a tape of weird droning sounds. I found a comfortable spot on the floor, rested my head against a plant, pulled my hat over my eyes and quickly fell asleep. But I think my snoring kept everyone from entering the new dimension, because when I finally woke up, a few people were staring daggers at me. After making a polite but hasty departure, I promptly crossed mind control off my list.

The love that had been deposited within me kept yearning for a soul mate, but I didn't know where to find one. The words *love* and *peace* were blowing into 1969 like balloons at a political rally, so it was pretty hard to determine what was real and what was not.

Consciousness was exploding at an alarming rate. You couldn't walk down the street without someone trying to entice you to expand your mind, but my mind didn't need expanding. I already knew the material world wasn't the real world, and I hadn't learned that from some guru. I'd learned it in the presence of God.

Whenever someone flashed me the peace sign, I immediately related it to the peace I'd experienced in heaven. I would watch everyone hug each other and think, "Yeah, they're into it. They know."

But they didn't. They spoke of love as if it was the exclusive property of our generation, but I knew love didn't come from us. It came from God.

In late September, I heard about a Vietnam War rally being held at nearby Kent State University. Since I'd just started driving again, I painted day-glo peace signs all over my '63 Chevy and took off in search of a noble cause. As I parked the car on campus and strolled toward the assembled crowd, I could hear a band playing and someone singing softly into a microphone:

C'mon people now, smile on your brother,
Everybody get together,
gotta love one another right now.

There was an unearthly quiet in the air, and I could have sworn the crowd was moving in slow motion. Many people were wearing black armbands as they marched solemnly down the street like mourners at a funeral.

I was amazed to see businessmen in suits standing right next to student radicals, and mothers with young children walking beside old men with white hair. I had never before seen this kind of unity in a crowd of such diversity. Everyone was speaking with one voice, and that one voice was simply saying over and over: "We don't want to kill people."

When the James Gang took the stage and led us all in chanting, "Give peace a chance," someone grabbed my hand and pulled me up on stage. While weaving back and forth in a human chain and gazing out on all the hopeful faces, I suddenly felt a great sense of belonging. At that moment, I truly believed we could change the world.

I held onto that belief throughout the winter as I recuperated from surgery, read spiritual books, and tried to create some kind of life for myself. Music was the ultimate social experience in 1969, so I started spending a lot of time in hip clubs and rock concerts.

There was a little coffeehouse/bar on the Kent State campus called J.B.'s, and that became my favorite place to hang out. One night when I went there to hear the James Gang, I found a note on the front door, saying, *Tonight: Glass Harp.*

I'd never even heard of this band, but when I walked in I was immediately blown away by their guitarist. Although not more than 17 or 18 years old, Phil Keaggy was the best guitar player I'd ever heard. From that night on, I made it a point to be in the audience whenever Glass Harp was playing.

Although I diligently tried to reclaim my life, it wasn't working. I was lonely, and the only people who hadn't forsaken me were druggies and outcasts. They genuinely cared about me, but they kept showing up at my door saying, "Hey, Mickey, I've got this good stuff . . . "

Drugs weren't a big draw for me, yet I desperately wanted to belong, so after awhile I chose to ignore the heavenly warnings I'd been given. Falling in with the only friends I could find, I exchanged the peace of heaven for a chemical high.

If smoking marijuana had been a light snack, then LSD was the feast everyone was waiting for. Acid was very fashionable with truth seekers who used it as a flashlight to travel deeper into the darkness. People were having spiritual encounters with this drug, and since I thought all such experiences were of God, I began to drop acid.

One night a bunch of us drove out from Cleveland to visit some friends who were building a huge house in the country. They were temporarily living in a summer cottage on the property and had invited ten of us over for a pleasant evening of recreational drug use.

As "In-A-Gadda-Da-Vida" blasted from the stereo, somebody took out a sheet of paper with little dots on it, tore it into individual pieces and handed them out like M&Ms. Everyone dutifully ingested their hit of acid, but when nothing happened within the next hour, we all automatically took another hit.

Seconds later, I noticed the house breathing with me. When people's shadows began dancing on the walls, I could hear hypnotic music coming from far, far away. And as my brain gently marinated in chemical soup, I let myself glide into the sparkling waters of euphoria.

But then everything tilted.

As human faces began melting into demonic masks, I could hear words of truth and words of torment spilling out of their mouths. I found myself too scared to talk and too paranoid to listen. All I wanted to do was escape. I had to get outside, but going outside didn't stop it.

The pure beauty of a starry night couldn't penetrate my fear. With increasing dread, I stuck a finger down my throat and tried to throw up the confusion, but the poison wasn't in my stomach. As the seconds rolled by like hours, I lay down on the grass and held tightly to the earth.

On the drive back to Cleveland the next morning, I tried to shake off the paranoia, but it was no use. There was no way to erase the things I'd seen or the terror I'd experienced. I felt like I'd just been spiritually raped. The drugs had stolen my innocence, and no drug ever created could give it back to me.

Chapter Seventeen

Giving Peace a Chance

It was New Year's Eve, the beginning of a new year, 1970, but I didn't feel much like going to a party. I'd just had a series of surgeries on my right hand, and was now dealing with severe pain and a huge wire sticking out of my bandage. As I lay on the couch that night with my hand propped up on my chest, I looked like a human UHF antenna.

Some of my friends decided to keep me company, and it wasn't long before our living room was overflowing with pizza boxes and bodies. Since this was my mother's house, everyone had to be on his best behavior. No joints, no LSD and no wastebaskets full of empty beer bottles.

My friends knew that I just needed to mellow out for the next few days, as the painful surgery had left me physically exhausted. I was still in a lot of pain as I quietly stared at the television.

Then someone got the bright idea of turning the TV volume down and turning up Jimi Hendrix on the stereo so we could all laugh as Guy Lombardo seemed to sing "Purple Haze."

Just six weeks earlier, the doctors had decided to reconstruct a hand out of my useless blob of fused fingers and frozen tendons. As if removing a glove, the surgeon began by stripping all the scar tissue from what was left of my right hand.

Next he hollowed out a small pouch of skin in the area between my breast and belly button, lined it with a piece of skin taken from my buttock, and then carefully laid my stripped hand inside the pouch. After covering it with the flap of chest skin, he then sewed the flap across my wrist and pulled tight to make sure it fit snugly.

This incredibly complex procedure took all day, resulting in extensive blood loss and intense pain. Immediately after surgery, my arm was packed and taped with enough gauze and wadding to totally immobilize it for the next six weeks.

The objective was to allow enough time for my body to manufacture new blood vessels in the forearm, which would then stretch and supply life-giving blood to the skin grafts. Although I looked like Napoleon for the next six weeks, the surgery was a success. After finally cutting the hand away from my chest, the doctor then stitched the transplanted skin all around and created something that looked like a child's boxing glove.

Then he began to move and manipulate the bones, fashioning fingers out of what was left and separating them from the thumb. After positioning a stainless steel wire to keep the fingers from growing together, the surgeon then wrapped it all up and sent me home to wait for the next operation.

That New Year's Eve, I casually laid my immobilized hand on a pillow on the couch. When a friend accidentally sat on my hand and bent the wire in it, I frantically tried to move the wire back into place. As I did, I noticed someone lying on the floor next to me, whispering: "Crucifixion!"

"Ohhhhhh . . . Cru . . . ci . . . fix . . . ion!"

I looked down and saw this guy who I knew had been studying Eastern religions and yoga. He was writhing in a weirdly sensual way, as if crucifixion was some kind of cosmic release or metaphysical pleasure.

"Cut it out, Eddie," I said with disgust.

"What's the matter, Mickey? You religious or something?"

"It's not funny."

No one paid any attention to me, so while Eddie continued his little performance, I got up and walked out of the room. Suddenly all these relationships seemed so offensive. Laughing at Guy Lombardo was one thing, but laughing at Jesus was another. It didn't seem right to me.

My friends were beginning to get on my nerves, so when Jerry asked me to drive with him to Florida for a February skydiving meet, I jumped at the chance. Jerry was one of the few old friends I had left, and we had an awesome time driving his Jaguar XKE through the beautiful mountains of Tennessee.

The eastern sky was ablaze and Jerry was fast asleep the morning we crossed over the Georgia state line to Florida. With the Beatles singing, "Here Comes the Sun," on the eight-track, I casually checked the rearview mirror before flooring the accelerator. Hurtling into the pure light of dawn at 145 mph, I felt this overwhelming assurance that my long, dark night was about to come to an end.

When I got home from Florida, the first thing I did was drive over to J.B.'s to hear Glass Harp. The three-piece band was amazing as always, but I kept noticing something different about Phil Keaggy. He had this big wooden cross around his neck, and he was playing hotter than ever. But there was something else. I could see light beaming from his face. Keaggy wasn't just singing about peace, he was radiating it, and I couldn't take my eyes off him.

The bar was filled with the usual blend of cool people, wannabe cool people and druggies. Through the fragrant haze of tobacco and marijuana smoke, I watched a young guy walk up to Phil and casually offer him a joint. It was the fashionable way to pay homage to a great musician, but he just smiled at him and said, "No, thanks."

That little interaction made Keaggy all the more interesting to me, and during the break we sat together on the pool table and shared a brief conversation. After noticing my mangled hand, he kindly held up a severed finger on his right hand and said, "Look . . . I got one, too."

Although he was quiet, Phil exuded this amazing intensity, but I just assumed that it had something to do with the recent death of his mother. I'd heard she'd been fatally injured in a car accident but had experienced some kind of encounter with Jesus shortly before she died.

His mother had been a devout Catholic, but that one experience radically changed her. And as I sat there talking to Phil, I could see it had changed him, too. Although he barely spoke about his mother, he looked me straight in the eye and said, "I used to do every kind of drug, Mickey, but I don't need that stuff anymore. I have Jesus now."

When he opened his Bible and read me some words about hope, I noticed a bunch of scribbled notes and underlines all over the page. I'd never seen anyone write in a Bible before. Phil wasn't just reading those words; he was studying them. But why? The Bible was just a historical book about Mary and the Crucifixion. What did it have to do with 1970? And what did it have to do with Phil Keaggy?

Although I listened halfheartedly, the words he was reading began to simmer inside me. Suddenly all the noise and smoke dissolved, and for a brief moment that bar became a very quiet place. Keaggy's openness prompted me to confess my loneliness, and as I began talking about my struggles, he tore a flap of cardboard off a nearby box and drew me a little map.

"Here's the address of a place where people are really living for the Lord," he explained. "It's a little Christian community on a farm in Mansfield, Ohio. Why don't you check it out?"

Not knowing how to respond, I quickly said, "Yeah, that sounds good. Maybe I'll try and get down there sometime."

As I tucked the piece of cardboard in my pocket, Phil said, "I gotta go," and walked back for his next set. As the band started to play, I looked around the room at all the people who were either high or trying to get high. And then I looked at Phil.

He wasn't just playing a gig; he was releasing music I'd never heard before. I didn't yet know the song of the Spirit, but I knew Phil Keaggy was singing it. And although that little map he gave me gathered dust on my bookshelf, I never threw it away.

By the spring of 1970, Kent State was rumbling like a volcano ready to blow. People were gathering to protest the bombing in Cambodia, and the campus was alive with dissent. Emotions were high as I made plans to attend another "peaceful" demonstration. It had been six months since the fall rally, and I fully expected this event to be even more incredible than the last.

As I pressed my way through the crowd that early April afternoon, I could hear someone bellowing curses against the government over the loudspeaker. Just below the stage, there was a group of people shouting and holding up a papier-mâché effigy of Nixon draped with the American flag. As the crowd roared its rabid approval, I stared in disbelief as the flag-draped figure suddenly exploded into flame.

Who ARE these people? I thought to myself. This couldn't possibly be the same crowd I'd stood with on that stage last fall. These weren't pacifists. These were human hyenas biting and snarling and whipping each other into a frenzy!

As television cameras zoomed toward the stage and reporters frantically worked the crowd, I suddenly turned and walked away.

I don't want anything to do with these people, I thought to myself. *They're sick.*

On my way back to the car, I could hear the distant sound of hatred still echoing from the loudspeaker. As I sadly drove away from Kent State, I mentally crossed the peace movement off my list.

When I got home that night and turned on the television, I caught the last part of an interview with a musician who'd become one of my cultural heroes. When the subject of Vietnam came up, he told the interviewer, "Jesus Christ was the first nonviolent revolutionary." It all sounded so good, at least until some guy in the audience yelled something and the musician angrily jumped out of his seat.

I watched in shock as this self-styled pacifist ran over to the heckler and threatened to punch him. Right in the middle of his spiel on nonviolence, he got into a fight! I wearily switched off the TV and said to my brother, "All this hippie stuff about love and peace is a bunch of crap. I can't listen to it anymore." My list of things to believe in was getting shorter by the day.

The next weekend, I drove over to a party at my friend Doug's house. The Canadian parachute team was in town to practice for the world championships, and Doug was hosting a big spaghetti and beer feast for all the skydivers.

As I walked in, I could immediately hear the Americans and Canadians engaging in their favorite pastime: one-upmanship. Crude putdowns had always been part of competition skydiving, but it was getting harder and harder for me to deal with all the cocky attitudes and sarcastic remarks. However, one of the Canadians had brought his German girlfriend along, and I immediately noticed how different she was from the rest of the team.

Walking over to her and extending my mangled right hand, I said, "Hi. I'm Mickey Robinson."

"Eva Hoffman," she said, smiling politely and taking my hand without looking at it.

"You don't exactly fit in with this bunch. Are you jumping tomorrow?"

"I'm not sure. I don't have my own gear."

"No problem," I assured her. "I won't be here in the morning, so you can use mine. And Doug probably has something you can borrow on Sunday."

Eva did jump on Saturday using my gear, and when I arrived at the drop zone on Sunday morning, she was already on board wearing a bright red jumpsuit and one of Doug's parachutes. We positioned ourselves according to jump order, and since Eva was going out before me, I sat a few feet behind her.

When I flashed her a reassuring smile, I noticed she looked kind of strange. I just assumed she wasn't that excited about jumping, and I couldn't blame her. My passion for the sport had also diminished, but I didn't want to lose my sky-diving friends. I figured Eva and I were jumping that day for the same reason—we both wanted to fit into this elite little group.

When it came time for Eva's jump at 4,000 feet, the pilot continued to circle slowly as he carefully watched her descent. Without a word, he motioned the next jumper out at 6,600 feet, and then I followed at 7,500 feet. But as I approached the gravel target, I noticed one of the female sky-divers sitting right on the spot where I wanted to land. I quickly pulled on the steering toggles and turned out sharply, but as I hit the ground, one of the wives came running up to me.

"What happened?" I asked, referring to the woman sitting on the target. "Did she get hurt?"

"No, it's not her . . . it's Eva! Her chute never opened!"

I quickly peeled off my harness and went running into the woods, assuming Eva had come in on her reserve and just gotten caught in the trees. But I was wrong. She had fallen from the sky without even hitting a branch, and her small body now looked as if it had never been alive.

She was lying face down on the ground, and when we turned her over, I could see a small ashen hand still gripping the main ripcord. As two men solemnly lifted her broken body onto a jeep and drove slowly away from the crowd, I spotted her boyfriend talking to another skydiver.

I stared at him in disbelief. Eva had just died trying to impress this man, yet he hadn't even taken the time to accompany her dead body. As members of the Canadian team began climbing back on board to resume their practice, I packed my gear and went home. I had no stomach for skydiving that day.

I later found out there was nothing wrong with either of Eva's parachutes; she'd just simply frozen in fear. This had been her 60th jump, but on her 44th, she'd experienced a ripcord malfunction. Although she'd been able to come in on her reserve that day, the frightening experience had marked her forever. Her heart was no longer in the sport, yet she knew she had to jump in order to belong.

Eva had swallowed tremendous fear to be part of her boyfriend's world, and in exchange for that privilege she'd paid the ultimate price. The memory of her blood red jumpsuit haunted me all the way home as I heard a Voice within me whisper, "She just wanted to belong . . . She just wanted to belong."

Though I'd already lost interest in jumping, I had continued to skydive until the day Eva was killed. Now I was beginning to realize how important it is to be committed to the right things in life.

On May 4, 1970, only five days after Eva's tragic death, my brother ran into the house shouting, "Did you hear what happened at Kent State? Turn on the TV!"

The screen was filled with mass hysteria, and the campus I knew so well was now overrun with weeping students, ambulances, National Guardsmen, and dozens of reporters.

The local newsman was frantically trying to describe how the Ohio National Guard had just opened fire on a group of protesters outside the ROTC building. Although the pressure had been building for days, no one had expected anything like this. The governor of Ohio had ordered the National Guard in to stop the escalating violence, but after the firebombing of the ROTC building, all hell broke loose at Kent State.

Four students were killed and several more seriously injured, but the death that was to affect me most was that of one of the young girls in the crowd. She hadn't even been part of that day's protest but had simply been walking by at a distance when a stray bullet struck and killed her instantly.

"That could've been me," I said quietly.

"What'd you say, Mickey?"

"I've been on that campus so many times. That could've been me lying there with a bullet in my chest." As I stared numbly at the television, I heard the Voice within say, "It's really important what you commit your life to."

The poets and prophets of my generation were still shouting about peace and love, but on May 4, 1970, I stopped listening. Eva had reached out for love, and those students at Kent State stood up for peace, but now they were all dead. Ironically, they'd been destroyed by the very thing they thought would set them free.

I didn't know what to believe in anymore, but I knew there was something beyond all the passion and fury of my generation. There had to be.

Chapter Eighteen

Hounded by Heaven

When I awoke that summer day in 1970, I knew something was different. As I rolled out of bed, I felt this strange sensation, as if ordinary events were being greatly magnified. Every song on the radio and every casual word had taken on divine significance. I couldn't even look out the window without being riveted by some profound revelation.

It was as if God Himself was letting me know that every earthly event was creating ripples in eternity. Throughout the entire day, I was being made to understand the tremendous power of human choice, and that understanding was causing me to tremble.

Conviction was closing in on every side as I paced back and forth in my living room that evening. Although the day had mercifully ended, there was no way I could go to sleep. My brain was still in overdrive when I heard my sister Barbara's Peugeot pull into the driveway.

She, my brother and our friend Eddie had just come back from a rock festival in Cincinnati. Barbara had already taken Eddie home, and as she dropped my brother off, I walked outside to hear all about the concert. But as I watched him slowly climb out of the car, I knew something was terribly wrong.

When he turned toward me in the eerie glow of a mercury vapor streetlight, an icy chill poured through me. This was the image I'd seen in heaven. His face was empty and, even though he was looking right at me, his eyes were hollow. As I looked questioningly at my sister, she just said, "He took a hit of PCP today."

Though normally used as an animal tranquilizer, PCP (ironically called *angel dust)* was becoming popular as a cheap and easy way to "blow your mind." I'd tried it a few times myself, but now as I looked at my silent brother, I knew it was a substance straight from hell. I wanted to shake him and yell, "Wake up!" But the drug had carried him far from the sound of my voice. I was practically sobbing as I touched his shoulder and said, "Hey, brother, how're you doing?" But he wasn't there.

I'd done nothing to stop this dreadful moment from becoming reality, and the sight of my brother's face now overwhelmed me with guilt. *You knew this was going to happen!* I thought to myself. *Why didn't you help him? Why weren't you a better example?*

Although it was 2:30 in the morning and my Chevy hadn't started for weeks, I had to talk to someone. In total desperation, I called a taxi and rode over to Eddie's house. When I rang the doorbell, Eddie slowly stumbled down the stairs and opened the door a crack.

I didn't even give him time to wake up before pouring out a frantic monologue about my brother and heaven and guilt and God. As Eddie sleepily leaned against the bottom of the stairwell and studied me through half-closed eyes, I watched in amazement as a shimmering one-inch band of pure white light began to outline his neck and head.

Eddie was a far cry from holy, so when he finally began to speak, I knew the words weren't coming from him. The more I listened, the more convicted I became, and that's when I realized the voice of God was speaking through my friend. When the band of light suddenly disappeared, the old Eddie emerged with a yawn and said, "Man, I'm really out of it. Can we finish this in the morning?"

As he made his exhausted way back upstairs, I went into the living room, lay down on the floor, and began to cry out, "God, I'm sorry, but I don't know what I'm supposed to do! Show me what I'm supposed to do!"

Suddenly a brilliant flash of white lit up the sky and, *Bbbooommm!* The house shook violently and the picture window vibrated above me as a bolt of lightning struck the tree in Eddie's front yard. As rain fell from the sky in torrents, I began to sob convulsively. And as I wept, shards of guilt and fear and shame began to float out on my tears.

When the front door opened twenty minutes later, Eddie's mom came running in, soaking wet. She'd been out with friends for the evening. Turning to hang up her raincoat, she saw me sitting on the living room floor and exclaimed, "Boy, it's really raining!"

Without getting up, I just looked at her and whispered, "Yeah, it's really raining." When she saw my tear-stained face, she politely turned and went upstairs, but by then it was all over. The cleansing tears were done and I was filled with a spiritual peace I hadn't known since those precious waking moments in Intensive Care. God had totally emptied me and then He filled me with this amazing joy.

When I awoke the next morning, I was elated to discover the peace was still with me, but it was accompanied by an incredible urgency. I wanted to change my life but I didn't know where to start.

I'll go to church! I thought. *The priest will tell me what to do.*

So I immediately got up, borrowed my friend's car, drove over to St. Michael's and knocked on the rectory door. Although the priests of my childhood were long gone, a man named Father Tyrone listened patiently while I gave him a mini-series version of my life.

I don't think he had any idea what he was in for, but I saw his eyebrows start to twitch as I described being burned alive and the radiance of heaven and Eva's death and my brother's face and God's endless pursuit.

When I glanced over at Father Tyrone, I saw that his hands were shaking. Although he was feebly trying to light up a Kool cigarette, I could tell my story was making him more and more uncomfortable.

"Then while I was lying on the floor," I continued breathlessly, "this huge bolt of lightning split the tree outside Eddie's window!"

Just then we heard a deafening *crack* as lightning hit the side of the rectory! Father Tyrone immediately leapt to his feet and yelled, "Oh, my God!" while knocking over his chair and sending his smoldering cigarette flying through the air. He then looked at me in terror, grabbed his chest and said, "I guess I'm not ready to go yet!"

The lightning hadn't phased me, so I kept talking a mile a minute as the priest started inching his way toward the door.

"So what do you think, Father?" I asked, trying to get some kind of an answer. "What do you think I should do?"

He quickly opened a drawer in the desk, took out a little catechism book and said, "Read this every morning and practice what it says." As he politely escorted me toward the exit, I turned around to say, "Isn't there something . . .?"

Father Tyrone had obviously had enough, because he interrupted me mid-sentence and said, "That's all I can do, son. I can't help you." Then he closed the door, and I was left alone in the hall with my little catechism book. I took that book home and devoured it, but when I turned the last page, I still didn't know what to do.

I didn't want to lose the brilliant peace inside me, so I passionately vowed not to do anything wrong. But this moral resolve lasted only a few weeks. The conviction and repentance wore off and I gradually went back to hanging out with all the wrong people in all the wrong places, caught up in the spirit of the age.

Goose Lake was one of those places. This Michigan rock festival was supposed to be another Woodstock, so my friends and I eagerly headed north to gorge ourselves on the musical feast. Yet as we drove into the festival I noticed that all the roads were named after drugs.

There were dozens of makeshift booths dispensing drug memorabilia, and it wasn't hard to see that everyone around me was busily snorting, smoking and swallowing anything they could get their hands on. As I stepped out of the car, I had to immediately dodge a naked man sliding through the mud on a watermelon rind. I thought, *Oh, my God, what have I done?* I wanted to leave, but my friends wanted to stay, and so I ended up trapped in a can of psychedelic sardines for the next three days.

I was beginning to feel like a yo-yo skidding dangerously between two worlds. Every time I took one step forward, I seemed to trip and fall two steps back. And whenever I made a decision to live above the weirdness, I was instantly surrounded by people intent on pulling me back. At least, that's what happened the night I went to J.B.'s with Barbara and her boyfriend.

We ran into Mark, an old classmate my sister hadn't seen since St. Michael's. As they rattled on about old times, Phil Keaggy walked over to our table and invited me to a prayer meeting later that evening. They listened politely while he talked to me, but when he walked away, they all looked at me in disbelief.

"You're not going with him, are you?" asked Mark sarcastically. "I thought you guys could come over to my place later. I've got this good stuff . . ."

"What would you rather do, Mickey?" asked my sister's boyfriend with a weird smile on his face. "Go to a prayer meeting, or get high?"

It didn't take long for me to get talked out of going to the prayer meeting. We all drove over to Mark's apartment, but I knew I'd made a big mistake when the conversation turned to religion.

"There's no heaven or hell! There's nothing but here and now!" explained Mark while blowing smoke in my direction. "Jesus had it all figured it out, and you can do the same, Mickey. You don't need these Jesus freaks telling you how to live!"

While they continued to lob spiritual volleyballs back and forth, I kept thinking, *I should have gone to the prayer meeting with Phil.* I couldn't believe how easy it was for me to get sidetracked.

Over the next few days, that old shadow of conviction was looming large, so when one of my brother's classmates invited me to his house for a Bible study, I made every effort to show up.

Although I was the token twenty-one-year-old in a roomful of teenagers, the kids were amazingly warm and welcoming. I actually felt pretty comfortable, at least until this guy named Steve started quoting from the Bible, and then I felt totally lost.

"Tonight I want to talk about this passage in Isaiah, *'All our righteous deeds are like a filthy garment . . .'* What do you guys think that means?"

As I glanced around at all the eager faces, I noticed I was the only one who looked dazed and confused. Steve might as well have been speaking Greek, but when I asked him for an explanation, he just smiled and invited me to breakfast with him the next morning.

"I don't understand this stuff about righteousness, Steve," I admitted between bites. "If a person's trying as hard as they can to do what's right, how come that isn't good enough for God?"

"Tell me, Mickey—have you ever done a good deed for someone or made what you felt was a morally right decision?"

"Sure," I answered confidently.

"Because you've done good things, would you call yourself a good person? A righteous person?"

"Yeah," I answered less confidently, remembering all the times I'd blown it in the past few months.

"Well, I can't say that about myself," he added with a surprising grin. "Even when I do good deeds, my motives are usually selfish. I want people to like me, or I want to impress some girl, or I want to get something in return."

"I've learned that selfishness is the universal human condition," said Steve, as he looked me straight in the eye. "I think you've learned that, too. But the story doesn't end there. God's made a way for us to exchange our selfishness for His righteousness, and that way is Jesus."

"I can't do this on my own, and neither can you," added Steve quietly. "The only way for us to stay clean is to stand under His mercy and live by His grace."

At first his words were mysterious and hard to understand, but they triggered something in me. And for some reason, I began to open up and tell Steve about heaven. I ended up telling him things I'd never told another human being. But right in the middle of my story, he began to laugh.

"What's so funny?" I asked, a little confused by his response.

"You have a ministry, man."

Because the only things I associated with ministry were celibacy and black robes, I immediately assumed he was talking about becoming a priest. Although I desperately wanted to pour love onto this parched and weary planet, I didn't want to wear weird clothes and hang out in dark confessionals. God was one thing. Ministry was another.

Besides, I was still busy with my full-time job as an outpatient. The doctor was in the process of rebuilding my nose using a section clipped from the back of my left ear, and the result was almost too perfect for my face. The doctor was extremely pleased with his creation, but when he gently pulled some packing out of the nostril a few days later, my perfect nose just fell to the floor!

And then there was the major renovation on my scalp. Two-thirds of my head was still covered with thick wavy hair, but much of the right side had been totally burned. When the doctor said he wanted to give me a more natural hairline, I didn't think it would be any big deal. He said I needed to be awake for the surgery, so they propped me up on a table and proceeded to numb my entire head.

The doctor surgically divided my scalp at the center and then pulled one side down, placing the hairline just above my right ear. This left an open strip along the top of my head (sort of a reverse *mohawk),* so the doctor cut a skin graft from my thigh and stitched it between the two sections of hair. I now looked like I'd been scalped by an Indian wielding a lawn mower. It felt even worse than it looked.

The idea was to move the bald area to the center so I could comb my hair over it. Though this seemed like a good idea at the time, the result was rather shocking. I thought my old scalp looked far better than this one, and when the anesthetic finally wore off, I was in mind-bending pain for the next three days.

I spent a long time recuperating from this radical surgery, and after four months of hanging around my mother's house, I was desperate for a change of scene. So when some friends asked me to join them for a weekend in Toronto, I jumped at the chance. The three of us drove up and rented a cheap room near the university. All the adjacent houses in 1970 looked like a neon version of Candyland.

Brilliant day-glo murals streamed across the sides of buildings, and I stopped to stare as we passed one house where the windows were painted like clown eyes and the front door opened into the center of a huge grinning mouth. This neighborhood was a far cry from the quiet suburbs of Cleveland.

After my friend Doug bought some hashish from students at a nearby dorm, we took off in search of a party. And when that party finally ended at four the next morning, Jim and I headed out into the frozen night looking for a hot cup of coffee. A deep winter chill had settled on the sleeping city, and as silver-dollar-sized snowflakes floated through the air, we spotted a little psychedelic coffee shop on the corner.

I felt a buzz just walking in there. Even at four in the morning, the room was alive with intellectuals blowing smoke rings and black-light posters pointing the illustrated way to infinity. The place was perfect for doing illegal and cosmic things, so as the sound of a sitar merged with the hiss of espresso machines, Jim rolled us a breakfast joint of tobacco and hash.

When we walked back out into the icy streets, Jim and I slowly passed the joint between us. Just as we turned a corner, I spotted a guy standing twenty yards ahead of us on the sidewalk. Even with his back turned, I could feel there was something different about him.

Although I couldn't see his face, I watched the giant snowflakes melting in his long brown hair. The man suddenly turned and looked right at me.

I knew instantly this was Jesus. His eyes were filled with amazing love and terrible sorrow, yet I felt no condemnation. His expression was calm and serene, like the face in some ancient painting, and as He locked me in His gaze, for one eternal moment the rest of the world seemed to disappear.

I shamefully averted my eyes as we walked past him, but then I nervously whispered to Jim, "Do you think we should have offered him the J?" Just as I said that, my voice echoed backwards from another dimension, as if God was stopping time to let me hear myself speak.

"Well, you're holding the J, Mickey," answered Jim in a weird mocking tone of voice.

When we got back to the room, I couldn't speak for the next 36 hours. My troubled thoughts ricocheted wildly between earth and eternity . . . right and wrong . . . good and evil. The look of disappointment I saw on Jesus' face shocked me.

My roommates didn't even notice my silence. They were just interested in themselves, and as they continued their mindless chatter, I became increasingly uneasy. In my highly sensitized state, their cynical words began to sound almost evil. I'd gone to Toronto to have a good time with these guys, but now I couldn't wait to get away from them. And on the drive back home to Cleveland, I felt lonelier than ever.

Just a few weeks later, I found myself sitting on a gymnasium floor in Akron, Ohio, surrounded by 1,000 electrified people. Phil Keaggy and Glass Harp had been steadily gaining popularity. I'd come hoping to throw off the desolation that had plagued me since Toronto, but it was no use.

When the lights finally dimmed and the sound of Phil's guitar soared into the gymnasium, everyone around me went bananas. I closed my eyes and tried to melt into the music, but it was no use. I couldn't feel anything. As if imprisoned in a see-through box, I could no longer hear, taste or touch the world around me.

All my senses were numb. It was then I fearfully whispered, "God, please help me. No one knows or understands what I'm going through. There's no one I can even talk to about the things that keep happening to me. I'm totally alone."

Just ten seconds after I prayed that prayer, someone laid two incredibly gentle hands on my shoulders. When I opened my eyes, I saw a young girl with long brown hair and bell-bottoms. She was standing there with tears streaming down her face and I heard her say, "God, he's so beautiful. Take him deeper."

Suddenly I could feel again. As small waves of love began to wash against me, I was filled with a calm so deep I could barely sit up. And then I heard that Voice within me saying, "I understand you, Mickey, and I know everything about you." Someone greater than all my circumstances knew me and I was now aware that He was with me!

When I opened my eyes, the young girl was gone.

But I was no longer alone. I knew God was with me.

Chapter Nineteen

Man Tends . . . God Mends

When my doctor walked into the hospital room early one morning in 1971, I was under the covers pretending to be asleep. He and I had decided to play a little joke on his colleagues, so as he started rattling off some complex medical jargon, I carefully reached behind the bed and flipped the light switch that turned on my black light. When I suddenly threw off the covers and bolted upright, they all stared as if I was Dracula rising for a snack.

I'd been stuck for several weeks in this sterile room, and had just finished doing some redecorating. After bringing in a bunch of posters and hanging them under a swag of purple fabric, I'd secretly exchanged my regular bulb for a black light. When I turned it on, my boring cubicle was instantly transformed into a nice little psychedelic lounge.

Although I was being forced to endure one more long stay in the hospital, I was no longer willing to act like a patient. I wanted everything to feel as normal as possible, so I casually wandered the halls in cut-offs and T-shirts. Then in the afternoons, I would sit quietly on the bed and strum my guitar for hours while sending healing vibrations into my bandaged hand.

I'd been reading the Bible since my conversation with Steve, and had even started praying regularly. I earnestly prayed, "Lord, I don't want to hurt anyone, and I don't want anyone to hurt me. If you've got someone special, please send her my way."

I still hadn't found "her," even though I had seen a couple of girls in the past year. One of the relationships was totally casual, but Laura seemed to be getting pretty serious about me. We did share a mutual interest in God, but Laura was sort of a walking, talking dish of spiritual minestrone. Although our talks were challenging to my soul, I was starting to get a weird feeling in my spirit.

"How do you know good isn't the flip side of evil, Mickey? Maybe God and the devil are one," said Laura matter-of-factly. "I don't even believe in death anymore. I think we're just going to keep on evolving until we reach higher consciousness."

Laura was leaving herself open for greater revelation and was always studying some new book on spirituality. She often tried to pass them along to me, but when I cracked one open for a closer look, I felt a cold wind blow across my soul. We were definitely headed in different directions.

One night as we walked arm-in-arm through the dark city streets, headlights from a passing car threw our shadows against a wall. As the car passed and the two shadows merged into one, Laura eagerly pointed and said, "Mickey, I think that's some kind of sign. Looks like we're going to be together forever!"

Just as she finished speaking, that familiar Voice within me whispered, *You cannot go on with this person.* I knew I wasn't in love with Laura, and that little warning finally prompted me to end the relationship.

In the spring of '72, I was definitely at a crossroads, and after being released from the hospital I knew it was time to find a job.

I took a temporary job driving a taxi. I thought it would keep me out of trouble and provide a little extra money, but I had no idea it would become the perfect way to preach my gospel of non-violence. While driving through suburban traffic day after day, I tirelessly campaigned for peace, love, McGovern and Jesus.

I kept my acoustic guitar in the front seat, and in-between fares I would strum chords, talk to God, and sing, "We are stardust, we are golden, and we've got to get ourselves back to the garden." That song quickly became my statement of purpose. No matter what had gone down in the past, I still believed in the utopian dream of a world without war.

I was so busy delivering my *Sermon in the Cab,* I completely ignored the cruder aspects of my job. Whenever a businessman asked me to find him a prostitute, I just smiled innocently and started talking about a cease-fire in Vietnam.

As I continued to study the multitudes climbing in and out of the back seat of my cab, a Beatle's song kept playing over and over in my mind: *Ah, . . . look at all the lonely people.*

One of my regulars was an elderly woman who could hardly afford the $1.50 cab fare, yet she was too old and too frightened to take the bus. While driving her to the grocery store week after week, my heart began to break for the many lonely people in America.

I saw them all in my rearview mirror: the rich, the poor, the successful, and the scared. I soon became a captive audience for women who needed someone to talk to, and a confessional for men desperate to lighten their load of guilt.

As the human circus rolled by day after day, I began to see people as God sees them. And as my human compassion was being stretched, I read the Bible and played my little songs to God. That growing relationship with God was the best part of my life. Still, I yearned to make connection with others who believed.

When I found out Phil Keaggy was going to be playing in a church on the east side of Cleveland, I knew I had to go. Although Glass Harp had just recorded their third album and was on the verge of making it big, Phil had suddenly dropped out to form an acoustic duo with Peter York. That seemed like a weird thing to do at the time, but later he explained: "I don't want to be a superstar. I just want to praise God."

Because my friend Bill was a virtuoso guitarist, I asked him to come with me to the concert. After climbing into my car that snowy night in October, we courageously made our way through the blizzard on four bald tires.

When we walked into the church and sat next to a lady with five squirming kids, Bill gave me a funny look. I was beginning to think we'd made a mistake, but when the music started, I knew I was in the right place.

Phil was no longer trying to please an audience, but was now playing his music for God and God alone. I'd never experienced real worship before, and as I sat there listening, the chords swept over me like the wind at 12,000 feet—clean and pure and full of light.

"Whaddya think?" I whispered to Bill, who was sitting there with a dreamy look on his face. He hated anything that smacked of religion, but he loved this man.

"Well, it's not Glass Harp," answered Bill, "But the vibes are incredible!" Neither one of us could explain the raw joy in that room, but both of us could feel it. I had a hard time remembering I was in church.

Although I experienced something powerful at that concert, the presidential election was only a few weeks away, so I quickly turned my attention back to the fate of America. As I drove my taxi and scattered my seeds of non-violence, I felt like I was making a vital contribution. But all of that changed the day Richard Nixon was elected.

I suddenly realized that the noble cause was dead in America. My peace balloon had just been shot down, and I wasn't about to spend the next four years trying to re-inflate it. Why waste time and energy on a system that was never going to change?

The power mongers were still in charge of America, so the only logical thing left to do was drop out. I would live in a geodesic dome on some remote island, grow my own vegetables, be incredibly nice to everyone, sing poetry to God and mind my own business.

This made even more sense after I discussed the fate of planet earth with my old friend Jeff, a Vietnam vet who'd been talking to a sociology professor at a nearby college.

"This guy says we've only got five to ten years before a nuclear meltdown. But if we head for a place where the wind doesn't blow," Jeff added cheerfully, "there's a chance we might survive."

I said to him, "I don't know about you, but as soon as my settlement comes through, I'm buying property and moving to Jamaica."

All during that winter of '72-'73, I drove my taxi and dreamed about paradise. I just assumed I'd be going there alone, but everything changed the night my friend Jimmy invited me to play cards at his friend's house in the suburbs of Cleveland. Although I didn't know the girl giving the party, Jimmy told me, "You've got to meet this chick, Mickey."

It was a cold February night, and as I stood on the porch shivering in my Italian Eskimo coat, a slim girl with long blonde hair carefully opened the front door.

"We made it!" said Jimmy, grabbing my hand and pulling me into the warm house. "Mickey Robinson, meet Barbara Newport."

Although I could tell she was rather shy and insecure, I was immediately drawn to her beautiful smile. And there was something else. Whenever I met new people, they usually spent the first few minutes staring at my face. But Barbara was different. She didn't even notice my scars.

"You can put your coat in here," she said quietly, opening a bedroom door and motioning to a chair already piled with coats. As the two of us stole a quick glance at each other, I noticed a small poster on the wall behind her. Looking closer, I realized it was inscribed with a quote from Walden: *Our lives are being frittered away by detail. Simplify.* Thoreau was one of my favorite thinkers, so for the rest of the evening, I studied Barbara Newport with increasing interest.

Her parents were out of town, so she'd invited a bunch of friends over to hang out and play Crazy Eights. Although she was a freshman in college, I quickly concluded that school was not her thing. She was like most nineteen-year-olds in America, trying to stay afloat within a cultural sea of free love, easy drugs, and shifting values.

Her current boyfriend was there that night, but his presence didn't hinder what was happening between us. As the evening progressed and our attraction increased, everyone else in the room seemed to disappear.

When I got home, I immediately called her on the phone and we talked until dawn. As we began to spend time together, I was reintroduced to emotions I hadn't felt since before the accident. Although we'd just met, I knew Barbara was someone special.

She felt the same about me, but her parents were a different story. I wasn't exactly the Prince Charming they'd envisioned for their daughter, and as our relationship deepened, they grew more and more uptight.

When Barbara and I drove down to Florida and then flew to Jamaica in March of '73, I told her about my big plan to bail out of the states. I didn't know what her response would be, but I wasn't surprised when she said, "I'm with you, Mickey." Barbara didn't seem to care what we did, as long as we were together.

By now we were crazy in love, and although we wanted to make a lifelong commitment, neither of us cared about religious ceremonies or man-made institutions. Because our relationship was spiritual, we felt no need to make it legal, so we simply married each other in the presence of the wind, the waves, and the Lord.

After finding a magnificent stretch of white sand beach, we waded out into the sparkling blue ocean in our cut-offs and T-shirts. When we were waist-deep in the water, I picked Barbara up in my arms and slowly spun around in a circle while we pledged to love each other forever. Then we joyfully hugged and kissed and laughed and dove into the water like Tarzan and Jane on their honeymoon. We felt invincible. Nothing could touch us now.

But on the drive back to Cleveland, we decided to keep our little ceremony a secret. Barbara's parents weren't ready for our "marriage," so we just moved back into our respective homes and waited for the right moment to break the big news.

A few weeks later, I took Barbara with me to another Phil Keaggy concert. As always, the music was incredible, but toward the end of the evening, Phil started talking about commitment.

"Some of you just like to sit around and talk about Jesus," said Phil, "but you can't do that forever. Sooner or later you've got to make a decision. Is He just some enlightened being, or is He Lord? There are a few of you out there tonight who need to stand up, leave everything behind and surrender your lives to Jesus Christ."

I instantly knew he was talking to me, but for some reason, I seemed to have a ton of lead in my pocket. Although I was usually the boldest guy in the room, I felt strangely apprehensive. Yet as the seconds ticked by, I began to feel a tremendous heat, and when Phil said, "Who wants to stand up for Jesus?" my body felt like it was on fire.

When I finally managed to break through the invisible barrier and get out of my seat, I realized Barbara was the only other person standing, and when she smiled up at me with a look of complete trust, I knew she was simply following my lead.

Even though I didn't understand what it meant to surrender to God, I knew I wanted to experience more of Jesus. And as I stood there in that auditorium, I began to feel this tremendous relief, as if some immense weight was being lifted off me. When Phil saw me standing, he gently nodded in my direction and said, "Thank you, brother."

As I stood there basking in this radiant moment of commitment, I had no idea how hard it was going to be to hold onto this mustard seed of faith, especially when I had to face the inevitable showdown with Barbara's parents just a few days later.

They had decided to move to Washington, D.C., and since they expected their daughter to move with them, Barbara had to tell them about her *marriage* to me. Their response was less than enthusiastic, and in a last-ditch attempt to split us up, Barbara's father threatened to disown her. But it didn't work. We were determined to cling to each other no matter what.

On the same day Barbara's father issued his ultimatum, I had to go back into the hospital for another complicated surgery on my hand. Although the procedure went pretty smoothly, my regular doctor was called away immediately following the operation. Since the head resident was also out-of-town, my case was temporarily assigned to some first-year-resident.

I'd had the surgery on Wednesday, and by Friday I could feel that the dressing on my hand needed to be changed. I kept asking for the doctor, but when no one showed up I decided to take matters into my own hands.

I'd long ago learned how to change my own bandages, so when the hallway finally quieted down on Saturday night, I carefully snuck into the nurse's station and stole a suture kit. But a nurse stopped me on my way back to my room and I had a hard time trying to explain my predicament.

"My bandage needs changing, but no one will listen to me!" I complained in complete frustration.

"The doctor will be in to see you Monday morning, Mr. Robinson," said the nurse as she confiscated my stolen supplies.

"You don't understand! Monday will be too late!" I said frantically.

"You need to go back to your room now," she said with a firm voice and a cold stare.

The situation was hopeless. There was nothing I could do about my hand, and when I called Barbara and asked her to come to the hospital, she tearfully said, "My dad doesn't want me to see you, Mickey. I'm going to try and change his mind, but I can't come today."

I was feeling desperate and abandoned, but when I called my mother to find human comfort, she had an emotional re-action over the phone. When I finally hung up, I felt just like a turkey at a target shoot. Bullets were flying everywhere, so I simply lay down in defeat and waited for the inevitable.

When the doctor finally showed up Monday morning and began to unwind the bandage, I watched in horror as all the delicate skin grafts slid right off into his hand. The painful surgery was now a total loss, and the embarrassed doctor could barely look me in the eye.

As I sat there quivering with frustration and rage, I whis-pered, "Is there someplace I can go to be alone?"

"We have a chapel on the first floor," answered one of the nurses in a compassionate voice. "There's usually no one there this time of day."

Without another word, I quickly left the room and walked down the stairs. When I flung open the wooden doors of the chapel, I immediately sank to my knees in despair. I lay on that cold hard floor and cried until I couldn't cry any-more, and when I finally opened my swollen eyes, I found myself staring at a huge mural on the wall.

It was one of those gentle old depictions of Jesus teach-ing his disciples, and as I studied it for a moment, I noticed something written underneath. Squinting my eyes in the dim light, I read: *Man tends . . . but God mends.*

As those five words leapt out at me like a flame in the wind, I suddenly knew there was no one on earth who could fix me. God and God alone was my healer, and no amount of human bungling could mess up His plan. Although I still didn't know what He wanted from me, I was beginning to understand the meaning of the word *surrender*.

Chapter Twenty

Nowhere to Hide

Things were definitely coming together. Barbara's parents had finally left for Washington, D.C., so she and I quickly moved into our own apartment in downtown Cleveland. A friend of ours rented us his dingy little second-floor apartment with no refrigerator and no stove, but we didn't care. We had a bathroom, borrowed dishes, some broken-down furniture, lots of candles . . . and each other. That was all that mattered.

This crummy apartment was actually our honeymoon cottage. Every day we strolled hand in hand through the streets of Cleveland, stopping at Central Market to buy our daily ration of cheese and bread. Then in the evenings we'd hang out with friends, play music, smoke dope, read *Mother Earth News,* talk about God and dream about our Jamaican utopia.

Although Barbara and I were finally together, I still didn't feel like I belonged anywhere. The truth seekers were daily abandoning their search for political justice, and all the peace people were now disappearing into the hills to build their cabins and plant their beans. As a result of this exodus, the counterculture was now made up of drug users, drug sellers and burned-out hippies.

On the flip side were the materialists, the capitalists, and anyone who trusted the system. As far as I was concerned, the culture and counterculture were both weird, and I didn't belong to either one. The noble cause was dead, so I had to stake my claim, build my dome, and live far away from the clutches of social disillusionment.

In September, I finally received the long-awaited insurance settlement from the accident, and although $60,000 wasn't really that much, it seemed a veritable fortune to Barbara and me. This was our big chance to escape Ohio, so we immediately flew to Jamaica to purchase our little chunk of paradise.

Even though I wanted to drop out of America, I had no desire to drop out of mankind. As soon as we got to Jamaica, I started thinking about building an Orange Julius stand and taking people parasailing in the bay. I just didn't want to get eaten by a dog-eat-dog society, so I started making plans to pursue peace, love and parasailing in my little portion of the planet.

When a realtor told me about 107 acres for sale fifty miles from Montego Bay, Barbara and I took a few of our new acquaintances and drove up north to make a day of it. As we walked around the lush acreage studded with banana and mango trees, I began to draw a mental blueprint for my kingdom by the sea. This place was absolutely perfect: a 20th century "Garden of Eden" with the Caribbean for a backyard. Plus, I could easily recoup my investment by subdividing half the property into small lots.

As the realtor led us down a steep mountain path overlooking the ocean, my mind was exploding with possibilities. Everyone went on ahead, as I stopped for a moment to check out a possible site for my dome. I was so overwhelmed by the beauty that I said out loud, "So this is paradise!"

The minute those words left my mouth, I stopped dead in my tracks. This was the place I'd seen in the heavenly vision. The path, the sunlight, the flowers . . . even my words were exactly the same! But as my heart started to beat wildly, I heard that familiar Voice within me say, "There is no paradise on earth. There is no utopia, and there is no going back to the garden."

A prickly dread crept over me and I walked down toward the others. Barbara was laughing about something, but when she saw my face, her expression radically changed.

"What's wrong?" she asked cautiously.

"I'm not sure. I'll talk to you about it later."

In the natural, everything had just fallen into place, but in the spiritual, something was very, very wrong. God had just declared my "Garden of Eden" off-limits, and all those bananas and mangos were now forbidden fruit. Although my logical mind told me to hang onto this piece of property, my spirit was warning me to let it go.

I was haunted by an eerie sense of foreboding, and that night I finally said to Barbara, "I don't think this is what God wants me to do." Although I didn't go into detail, she could easily see how shaken I was. I knew everybody was going to think I was a total flake for letting go of that land, but I just wanted out. My tropical "Walden Pond" had suddenly become a nightmare, so Barbara and I packed our bags and flew home to Ohio.

It was pretty hard to return to that dingy apartment. We were both feeling displaced, so after buying an Irish setter puppy named Abraham, we started talking about moving to the country. There was just no way to live a cozy inner-city existence with our furry new child. On the day he leapt from the second-floor window in an attempt to follow us to the store, we knew it was time for a change.

So, in December of 1973, we became the proud owners of an old Victorian farmhouse, a hand-hewn barn and eight snow-covered acres in Ashland, Ohio. Neither one of us had ever even grown a radish in a Dixie cup. But Barbara and I were ready to make our mark as the great American farm couple.

Apparently I'd watched too many reruns of "Bonanza" because as soon as we moved in I started thinking we needed more land. After the nice people down the road sold us six more acres, we adopted a lifestyle that was somewhere between *Green Acres* and *Alice's Restaurant.*

Although I had no idea how to organize my little McFarm, I instinctively knew that every farmer had to own a truck, so I bought an old Dodge pickup and started hauling furniture home from the second-hand store. Since we were living in a Victorian house, our decor naturally had to look heavy, wooden, dark and distressed.

As we busied ourselves with the oddities of rural living, I quickly realized that heat had to be our number one priority. Although we had to spend most of our time near the stove that December, I was determined to make our first Christmas together a memorable one. We were going to rejoice greatly, despite the fact we were freezing to death.

One afternoon, while Barbara was taking a nap, Abraham and I snuck out of the house, jumped into the old Dodge and headed for town. I'd never bought a Christmas tree before, so I naturally picked out the tallest and most expensive one I could find (a $22 Douglas fir). It was truly majestic, and looked like it would reach to the very top of our high ceiling. Actually, that tree ending up blocking the entire bay window, but what we lost in scenery we made up for in pine needles.

After Barbara and I used up 12 boxes of tinsel, we threw ourselves a little housewarming party. We ate popcorn, drank hot chocolate, oohed and aahed over our little presents, and basked in the glow of domestic bliss. It was a happy time for us.

Since there wasn't much to do during those cold months of winter, we entertained friends from the city almost every weekend. Our house soon became official party headquarters, and with all the music and laughter, there wasn't much opportunity to get lonely. But when the snow started to melt, I began reading seed catalogues and having daydreams about amber waves of grain.

After we bought a tractor and some other farm equipment, Barbara told me about her lifelong dream—that of owning a horse. That dream was within our grasp, so we purchased our first real farm animal, a little red quarter horse we named "Shannon."

One day while I was rattling around on my tractor, Barbara came up behind me and said, "Mickey, she's lonely."

"Who's lonely?"

"Shannon. She needs a friend. We need to get another horse to keep her company."

A lonely horse is a terrible thing, so back we went to her farm of origin, trying to find a four-legged playmate for Shannon. I, too, had once dreamed of owning a shining stallion, and in my mind this wondrous creature was named *Cherokee.* I'd long since forgotten that boyhood fantasy, but when I spotted a lone Appaloosa grazing in the field, it all came rushing back to me.

"Is that one for sale?" I motioned eagerly.

"She could be . . . for the right price," answered the owner.

"What's her name?"

"Cherokee."

This was my horse of destiny, so we gladly paid the money and welcomed another creature to our collection. I thought I was just buying a horse; I had no idea I was actually acquiring a four-legged therapist, prayer partner, and friend. It was as if God Himself had chosen Cherokee to lead me through a miraculous new phase of rehabilitation.

Nonviolence still lay at the heart of everything I believed, so I naturally wanted to train her without inflicting any pain. I found that by just using a halter, two lead ropes and voice commands, I was soon able to teach my amazing horse how to turn tight figure eights.

Her ancestors had belonged to the Nez Perce Indians, and I was constantly amazed at the passionate heart and sensitive spirit that had been bred into her. The life in that horse inspired life in me, and riding her gave me back the vitality I'd lost in those long years of hospitalization.

Every time we galloped into the sunrise or sunset, the very heavens opened up for me, and soon all my prayers were being prayed on horseback. Although I'd always loved the magnificence of the sky, Cherokee introduced me to the beauty of the earth. In the night, in the snow, in the sun, in the mud, and in the rain, the two of us roamed together across the gentle farmlands of Ohio.

Not long before, ı had taken a job working as a night watchman at Ashland High School, and when I came home every morning at 6 a.m. I automatically headed straight for the barn. Those dawn rides felt like freedom itself, and as my legs gripped Cherokee's powerful sides I could literally feel strength pouring back into me.

When the first wildflowers appeared that April, they seemed to represent the springtime of my life. It was as if I'd been raised from the dead and was seeing everything for the first time.

Standing by our rusty gate one warm spring morning, I breathed in the scent of lilacs as I watched Barbara walk toward me down the narrow path. Then when she smiled at me, I suddenly remembered.

Heaven. Barbara was the woman I'd seen in heaven! The rusty gate, the narrow path and the smell of lilacs were all part of my vision. Despite all the twists and turns of the past six years, I had somehow stumbled upon my destiny, and it was good.

Although God told me there was no such thing as paradise on earth, I still wanted to create some little corner of peace and tranquility. I wasn't supposed to plant a garden in Jamaica, but maybe it was okay to plant one in Ohio!

Since I had two magnificent piles of decomposed manure, I bought a spreader and began to cultivate a garden worthy of the Jolly Green Giant. Having absolutely no concept of size or yield, I started with a mere 84 tomato plants!

It didn't take long for me to become an expert manure spreader, and pretty soon Barbara and I were living the zucchini-eating, peace-loving, mud-luscious, earth-mother type of existence. While I compulsively plowed and messed around in the dirt, Barbara faithfully peeled and strained and stewed and canned.

Although it was easy to impress friends with my born-again farmer routine, I was beginning to feel restless, and I didn't know why.

Barbara and I were beginning to spend a lot of time with a Christian woman we'd met in Cleveland. Although I was reading the Bible regularly, we still weren't involved in any small groups, so Joan kindly took us under her wing to teach us the fundamentals of faith.

Although I was incredibly hungry for spiritual truth, Barbara just didn't seem to have as much of an appetite. She wasn't as confident to pursue God on her own as I was, but she was more than willing to follow me, even though I was still a wanderer in the wilderness.

Night after night I had strange dreams that woke me out of a sound sleep. The dreams symbolized my spiritual dehydration, but I didn't want to admit that to myself or anyone else. Although music had always been a deep well of inspiration for me, the buckets were starting to come up empty. Not even the guitar could rouse me from my desolation, and because every song was beginning to sound the same, I just stopped singing.

I'd always been so passionate about everything, but nothing ever seemed to satisfy my wanting soul. Even riding Cherokee could no longer soothe my spirit. I wanted to be cosmic, and I wanted to be Christlike, but sitting on that fence was becoming more and more uncomfortable.

I was finally ready to admit that I wasn't cut out to be a farmer. God was right. Utopia was nothing but a figment of my imagination. I was more into people than I was into organic gardening, but what kind of career and lifestyle could really fulfill me? Guys like me usually become talk-show hosts, politicians, or used-car salesmen, but none of those sounded very appealing.

My bank account was quickly depleting, and still I couldn't figure out what to do with my life. I couldn't even claim my identity as an outpatient anymore because I'd finally decided to end my rehabilitation career. There was only one more procedure that I wanted, and that was a cornea transplant.

Although my right eye had been blind since the accident, my name was taken off the waiting list for transplant donors in 1969. Because the eye was clinically dead, the doctors assured me that surgery would be a waste of time. But I wouldn't take "no" for an answer. I never stopped bugging them about the transplant. In an attempt to shut me up, they finally relented and put me back on the list.

One day while I was working in the garden, Barbara got a call from the hospital saying there was a cornea available. I immediately got myself psyched up, but just as we were about to walk out the door the doctor called back.

"The donor's too old, so we'll have to pass on this one," he said.

I was really disappointed, and just assumed I'd have to wait years for another donor. But only a few weeks later I received another call. A 29-year-old man died in a car accident right outside the hospital, and since the surgery had to be done within 24 hours, Barbara and I immediately drove up to Cleveland.

Dr. Thomas quickly set me up under a huge stereoscope, and after numbing my eye, proceeded with the delicate surgery. Using a thread thinner than a spider's web, he attached the new cornea to my eye by meticulously weaving 23 times back and forth around its edge.

After dressing it with an eye patch and a plastic shield, the doctor wrapped my head with another bandage and said, "I'll check this in seven days."

He didn't sound very enthusiastic, and I later learned that when he'd sliced off my old cornea, he'd found nothing there but a mass of scar tissue. The doctor thought this was all a waste of time, and even told his assistant, "The surgery won't make any difference, but at least he'll have his natural eye color back."

When the orderlies wheeled me into my hospital room, I asked them to block all window light. I had long ago learned to cooperate with the healing process by remaining very still, so I laid flat on my back with no pillow, requested complete silence, refused to eat and barely even moved for the next 72 hours. Although Barbara stayed faithfully by my side, I was in such an intense state of concentration that I barely acknowledged her presence.

The day Dr. Thomas came to check on me, I remained very still as he unwound the bandage, took off the plastic shield, and then very gently removed the patch. I had no idea what to expect, but when my dead eye perceived a faint ray of light, I whispered, "Oh, my God!"

"What's the matter?" asked Dr. Thomas.

"I can see!"

"I don't understand!" he exclaimed in total unbelief. "There's no possible way you should be able to see!"

"Well, I don't know how to tell you this, doc, but I can see two of you!"

Because the muscles were so weak, my eye kept floating around, reflecting two of everything, but that didn't bother me. I was ecstatic; my poor doctor was completely confused. He still had no confidence in the surgery, and because of all the scar tissue he wouldn't even risk removing the stitches for another six months!

I knew God had healed my eye, and when Barbara and I got back to the farm, the first thing I did was hop on Cherokee and ride bareback at break-neck speed. I was so overjoyed that I could barely contain myself. I'd been blind in my right eye for the past five and a half years, but now I could see perfectly! Although I'd just been given a powerful lesson in divine healing, I had no idea I was about to receive a powerful lesson in divine obedience.

The kingdom of God and the culture of man were both calling to me. But trying to walk both directions at the same time made me feel like I was losing my mind. Jesus was lord of my life, but He was not yet lord of my habits. Although I wanted to please God, I kept trying to please everybody else, too.

My spirit and flesh were at war. I wanted to choose something from Column A and something from Column B, and although this was okay inside a Chinese restaurant, it was not okay inside a Christian man.

Every time I read my Bible, I felt conviction coursing through my veins, but that feeling wasn't enough to keep me straight. Smoking marijuana wasn't that important to me, but I desperately wanted my friends' approval, so I followed the path of least resistance.

While waiting for my choices to get easier, I asked God to have patience with my double-mindedness, but by the fall of 1974 I was burning with conviction. Every time I'd open the Bible, a passage of Scripture would reach up and grab me.

Eventually, nothing felt good, nothing excited me, nothing was worth doing, and nothing made me happy. I didn't even care about my friends coming down on weekends. Barbara wasn't enough, my friends weren't enough, Cherokee wasn't enough, and the farm wasn't enough. I'd finally collided with an immovable object, and that object was God.

In February, my old friend Jerry invited Barbara and me to go on a vacation with him and his wife Kathy. I didn't have peace about going and, although I wanted to say no, my desire to fit in was still greater than my fear of God so I reluctantly said yes.

Jerry owned a Cessna 182, so the four of us flew down to Miami and then took a commercial flight over to Jamaica.

Because I had disobeyed God, I figured there was a chance I could die at any moment, and as I sat there envisioning another flaming plane crash, I became almost sick with fear. Refusing to eat or drink, I closed my eyes and silently begged for mercy.

The streets of Negril were full of people trying to make a buck, but when we passed one Jamaican man leaning up against a fence, he suddenly motioned for me to come near. I innocently walked toward him with a smile on my face. But when I approached him, evil words streamed from his mouth.

"Hey, you!" he screamed. "You didn't go to Vietnam, did you? You're a coward, and you deserved all that stuff that happened to you!"

I suddenly felt like I was lying naked on an operating table in hell. His words were a scalpel slicing me apart accusation by accusation, and for some strange reason, he knew exactly where to cut. Immediately, I figured out that he was into witchcraft and had the ability to read my mind accurately, mocking and accusing me.

I tried to placate his vileness with niceness, but it was no use. This man was like one of those picadors who repeatedly stab the bull. It's their job to weaken him for the final thrust of the matador's sword, and with every verbal jab, this man was draining my blood.

When I weakly turned away and ran to catch up with the others, I couldn't stop shaking. We stopped at a little cafe for breakfast, and I went into the bathroom to take a few deep breaths and splash cold water on my face. When I looked up from the sink, on the wall next to me was written: *"There is nothing sweeter than the name of Jesus."*

The conviction was burning so hot, I could barely keep it together. I kept thinking the ocean would revive me, so I ran down the Ocho Rios beach. I spotted a Rastafarian standing by the water. In a desperate attempt to wipe away the horror of my previous encounter, I walked over to talk with him, but when I got within a few feet, my blood turned to ice.

As he stared into my eyes, I felt a cunning evil trying to penetrate my brain, and when he started shaking a branch, I felt a terrible heaviness cover me like a shroud. I realized he was casting some kind of curse, and the next thing I knew, my feet were flying down that beach. I ran so fast my heart almost burst, and when I stopped to catch my breath, I noticed a piece of driftwood at my feet.

Cold terror crept over me as I remembered this exact scene from the heavenly vision I had seven years earlier, and I knew that if I turned around, I would be staring into the face of evil. Standing on that magnificent beach in the warm sunlight, I felt like I was standing at the gate of hell. As I started to shake uncontrollably, I made a frantic 180-degree turn and ran faster than I had ever run before.

I couldn't even speak for the next 24 hours, and when I prayed for mercy, I thought about how many times I'd asked God to forgive my disobedience. I knew God was able to deliver me from evil, but how many more chances was He going to give me? How many more wake-up calls would I get?

Chapter Twenty-One

I Surrender All

By the grace of God, I survived Jamaica, yet I was forever changed by what happened on that beach. The moment I finally turned and ran from evil, I knew there was no going back. Although I was dead broke and spiritually fried the day we boarded the plane for home, I was ready to do business with God.

Spiritual kindergarten was over, and I could no longer stall for time, make excuses, or bargain with God. On the flight back to Ashland, one question kept rolling over and over in my mind: "Are you going to live for Jesus, or are you going to live for yourself?" I had to choose between pleasing God and pleasing people, and I had to choose fast.

When we arrived at the farm, I was so grateful to be home I almost fell on my face and kissed the ground, but the moment we walked in the front door, the phone rang.

It was Barbara's mother, and the news was not good.

"Mickey, we've got to get there right away!" said Barbara. "My mom just had a blackout. She needs help."

Barbara was in a panic, so we got on our knees in the kitchen, prayed for her mother, and quickly made preparations to fly to Washington, D.C.

When we knocked on the front door, Barbara's mom opened it, took one look at us, and said, "What're you doing here?" I could tell that she'd changed her mind and didn't appreciate us coming so unexpectedly.

All of a sudden, our noble gesture seemed like a stupid idea, and when Barbara explained the situation to her father, he accused us of making a mountain out of a molehill. Our coming turned out to be a disastrous idea.

"I don't know what you're talking about, Barbara," he said briskly. "Your mother's fine, and she certainly doesn't need your help."

I could see it was no use, but because Barbara was so worried about her mom, I agreed to stay in Washington for the next few days. Little did I know Barbara's father was going to use every minute of that time to try and drive a stake into the heart of our relationship.

Day after day, he verbally pummeled his daughter, "You're 21, and you're going nowhere. You're a loser, and you're living with a loser. Neither one of you is ever going to amount to anything." And when Barbara's confidence finally hit an all-time low, he made his final bid and handed her the keys to a brand new yellow Vega.

I thought our relationship could withstand any kind of attack, but I was wrong. When we flew home, Barbara could hardly look at me. Her father's words had left her severely disillusioned, and within days of returning to the farm, she began packing her bags.

"Barbara, what are you doing? You know we belong together! This is our home!"

"I think we made a mistake, Mickey. I need to get away for awhile. I have to get my head together."

"Barbara, you're listening to a lie!" I pleaded. "You know God brought us together."

But I couldn't get her to hear me, and as I watched her drive away in her little yellow car, I had a sinking feeling I was about to be stripped down to nothing. Although my heart had been broken before, the pain of losing Julie was a whole lot less than the pain of losing Barbara.

When I walked back into the house, I could hear the empty echo of my footsteps. As I started to cry, Abraham lay down beside me and gently licked my hand. Our house was deadly silent, and for the first time in many years, I was left completely alone.

I kept calling Barbara at her parent's house, but I could tell she didn't want to talk to me. It was as if she had temporary amnesia, totally forgetting she had ever loved me.

"Barbara, I know it's God's will for us to be together."

"I'm not so sure about that anymore, Mickey."

"What do you mean?"

"I can't explain it. I just don't feel the same."

"It's the farm, isn't it? We don't have to stay here, Barbara! I don't care where we live—I just want us to be together!"

She would listen politely to my offers of undying devotion, but then make some excuse why it would never work. Nothing I said was getting through, and whenever I pressed the issue, I could feel her drawing farther and farther away from me. When she told me she was thinking of seeing someone else, I finally realized she had no intention of coming back.

Barbara had been gone about a month, and her absence left me plenty of time to think about my life. I was beginning to admit my failure as a husband and as a Christian. I wanted to blame Barbara for not getting straight with God, but what kind of example had I set for her? Even though I was good at quoting my Bible and lecturing her about Christ, I was far from being the man God wanted me to be. In all honesty, I fit perfectly the dictionary definition of a hypocrite.

My good guy image lay in shambles. I was a spiritual coward, and so it really didn't matter how nice I was, how cosmic my ideas were, or how many friends I had. God knew the truth about me. While claiming to love Jesus, I'd been a compromiser, and I was paying the price for my selfishness.

The Lord continued to show me my failure as a husband, but my friends kept telling me to put the blame on Barbara.

"You don't deserve to be treated like this, Mickey," they would say. "You're a good guy! Forget her, and find somebody else." But I wanted Barbara and no one else.

I was trying to be honest with myself, but I was yo-yoing wildly between God's dealings and my own emotions. When

I admitted my own failures, the Holy Spirit would gently counsel me, but every time I gave in to self-pity, the Voice within me grew strangely silent.

I yearned to hear that Voice, so every morning I drove to the six o'clock mass at a little Catholic church in West Salem. Even though the place was deadly quiet, there was a whole lot of shaking going on inside of me. I was reading my Bible every minute of every day and couldn't seem to eat, sleep or breathe without whispering some kind of desperate prayer.

I fasted, trying to empty my soul of its great pain, and after three days without food or water I put on my ski jacket and took off running across the hills. I was so physically numb that I barely noticed the freezing temperature. But when I finally sat down on a patch of dead grass beside our little creek, I collapsed in mental and emotional exhaustion.

All of a sudden, an evil presence began weaving a web of accusations in my mind, telling me I had caused my own accident . . . I had blown it by buying the farm . . . I had driven Barbara away . . . I had rejected God . . . I had screwed up my life.

This relentless flow of condemnation was so intense, I couldn't even think straight. I felt like a leper frantically trying to get close to Jesus, but every time I reached for the hem of His garment, an evil thought would kick me right back into the pit of shame. No matter how hard I tried, I couldn't break through to the grace of God.

The torment went on for seven hours as I questioned the motives behind everything I'd ever done. When I was finally ready, that calm, familiar Voice spoke words of life to me:

What you did was an act of love.

The minute I heard those words, the demonic accusations stopped, and something like a clean fresh wind cleared my soul of all oppression.

Suddenly, I realized how much I'd taken His love for granted. God had never forsaken me, yet I'd forsaken Him. I couldn't blame Barbara, the devil, or anyone else in the world for what was happening to me. I was the guilty one. I was the one who kept choosing to turn away from God. Although no one had ever spoken to me about repentance, I now felt an overwhelming desire to repent.

That's when I remembered something that happened on the playground when I was at St. Michael's. After watching my friend Eddie pin a little kid to the ground, I heard the boy cry out, "I yield! I yield!" The hair on the back of my neck stood up as I relived that scene in my mind. Quietly, as I knelt in the mud and bowed my head before God, I whispered the words "I yield."

And like a father receiving his wayward son, the Lord lovingly but firmly answered me: *If you want to be My disciple, Mickey, you have to be willing to follow Me without any guarantees. If you truly want to do My will, you're going to have to trust Me.*

I knew what I had to do, so I walked back into the house, knelt on the hardwood floor and prayed, "God, I release Barbara into Your hands. She doesn't belong to me, she belongs to You, but please don't let any harm come to her. Even if she never comes back to me, Lord, watch over her and protect her. Don't let her be destroyed."

Although Barbara was all I cared about on this earth, I finally understood that nothing could come before God—not even my beloved wife. The moment I released her to Him and prayed, *"Thy will be done,"* I became a true disciple of Jesus Christ. Little did I know that, at that exact moment some 400 miles away, Barbara was having her own encounter with God.

She had been seeking counsel from a Catholic priest, and that weekend he'd invited her to attend a retreat on a nearby farm. The retreat was sponsored by a monastic order of Catholic brothers, and at the exact moment I was releasing Barbara to the Lord, they were all gathering together for a spiritual exercise.

As Barbara stood with the others in a circle facing outward with her arms folded across her chest, she was asked to assume a posture of isolation, while singing "I Am a Rock." Then everyone in the circle was instructed to turn inside, unfold their arms, join hands together, fix their gaze upon another person and sing, "He Ain't Heavy, He's My Brother."

Although it was a simple exercise, something amazing happened to Barbara as she went through those motions. She was dramatically empowered by the Spirit of God. For the first time in her life, she surrendered her whole heart to God, and in the next few moments she was baptized in the Holy Spirit. Then the Lord so filled her with His joy and revelation, she wrote down a prophecy concerning our future life.

In an amazing set of divinely orchestrated circumstances, both Barbara and I surrendered to God at the exact same time. Although she'd been hiding behind me for a long time, God was calling her to step out of my shadow and into the light of Christ. The two of us had finally yielded to Him of our own free will, and although we once loved each other, we were about to learn how to love God first and draw upon Him to heal our marriage.

When I called her the next morning, the strange aloofness had disappeared. She asked me to come for her right away. When I heard her say the words, "I love you, Mickey," I bolted out of the house and headed straight for Washington, D.C.

Although her parents were totally dismayed when I showed up at their front door, the reunion between Barbara and I was worth every minute of pain. Because we had both chosen the Lord, the love we had for each other had become a thousand times greater, and as we stood there clinging to each other, I knew our commitment was forever sealed.

When we returned to the farm, everything seemed different. There was a new sense of peace in our relationship, as if some great war had just been settled.

Barbara started taking classes at the local community college and soon became friends with Juan, a Christian professor. God brought this man into our lives at just the right moment, and he quickly became a source of spiritual strength and wisdom. Juan was like our big brother in Christ.

Eventually, he challenged us about getting married within the church. Although we explained that our ocean vows in Jamaica had come from the heart, Juan said, "Yeah, I understand that, but are you brave enough to stand before the body of Christ and declare your faithfulness? Are you courageous enough to make that same commitment in front of your parents?"

We both knew that Juan was right, so we called our parents to invite them to our church wedding. On a magnificent fall day, Barbara and I were married in a private, quiet ceremony at the Catholic church in West Salem, Ohio. Barbara looked radiant as we pledged our love and commitment to each other. As we stood at the altar, I knew this was the happiest day of my life. And it was a time for all of us to experience an unusual peace together as a family.

Barbara became pregnant in June of 1975. She was elated, but I entered into a complete state of shock. For some reason, I'd never considered the reality of becoming a father. We'd always lived spontaneously from day to day, but with a child on the way, I had to get serious about the future.

I immediately found a job working in a plastic film company. Forty-two hours every week I organized the shipping area at Corko, and spent most of my paycheck fixing up the money pit we called a house.

Little by little, God reined me in and began fitting me with new responsibilities. Although I still loved riding Cherokee, our times together were becoming few and far between. One fall day, some neighbor kids came by to tell me there was something wrong with my horse.

When I followed them out into the field, I saw Cherokee lying dead on the ground. In an attempt to jump over the creek, she had somehow stumbled in the mud, fallen forward, and snapped her neck. As I knelt down beside my old friend, I tearfully asked, "Why God? Why did You let this happen? It makes no sense. Why did You let her die?"

I didn't yet understand that some of God's gifts are temporary. He had graciously given me Cherokee as a heart companion, and although she'd poured life into me on those awesome prayer rides, her purpose was completed. My years of spiritual isolation had come to an end, and I was being prepared to take my place within the body of Christ.

On March 4, 1976, our son Michael Richard Robinson was born in Ashland, Ohio. Because he was premature and weighed only 5.1 pounds, the doctor wanted to keep Michael in the hospital for a few weeks. Without consulting us, he arranged to give Barbara a shot so she couldn't breastfeed. When we discovered what he'd done, Barbara wept with disappointment. She desperately wanted to nurse our baby, and when we asked God to counteract the effect of the injection, He graciously answered our prayer.

Although we still weren't settled in a church when Michael was born, I'd been hearing about a place forty miles away called Grace Haven Farm. I figured Easter Sunday would be a good time to check it out, so we wrapped our son in blankets and headed for the sunrise service. When we pulled into the parking lot at Grace Haven, I couldn't believe my eyes.

In front of me was a scene I could only have imagined in my wildest dreams. I don't know what I expected, but this was a busy community of believers, young and old, who were joyfully serving the Lord. Barbara and I looked at each other in disbelief, as if to say, "Can you believe a place like this actually exists?"

The complex had basketball courts, dormitories, a chalet-looking building called The Lodge, a candle factory, and even a sandwich shop called The Yellow Deli. As I walked around with Michael in my arms, one guy greeted me with a bear hug.

These young Christians were following the teachings of Francis Schaeffer, a modern Christian philosopher. He had modeled the farm after his little community in Switzerland.

The chalet building was actually the church, and the dormitories housed kids from all over the world who had come for work-study programs.

The whole place was full of life, unlike anything we'd ever seen before. When we walked into the service, the room was packed with men with beards, bare feet, braids, T-shirts, guitars, flutes and radiant smiles. The incredible music went on for hours, and every few minutes someone would stand up and give an inspiring testimony or speak a word of grateful praise.

I usually had to fight boredom in church, but this was a far cry from boring. As I watched people loving on each other, hugging their kids, raising their hands in worship, and giving thankful testimony to the greatness of God, I knew we belonged.

If only I had accepted Phil Keaggy's invitation six years ago. This was the place he had told me about, but I'd had to travel a long and winding road to get here. At long last, Barbara and I had found a place where our mustard seeds of faith could safely grow.

Everything I'd ever dreamed of was on display here. Grace Haven was a huge community that shared everything in common, and it wasn't long before we joined one of their weekly home fellowships. In fact, we spent as much time as possible with the Grace Haven community. I still worked at Corko, but now I had a newfound joy in the Lord.

Worship was an integral part of life for the people at Grace Haven, and it wasn't long before their music became food for my soul. I hummed it, strummed it, sang it and began to spend every waking moment in a perpetual attitude of praise.

Barbara and I had finally found a fountain of spiritual life, and all we wanted to do was splash around in its refreshing water. My restlessness was gone and I was finally content to live on the farm, take care of my little family, and hang out forever with the people of God.

But one day in the fall of 1976, God turned His familiar spotlight on me once again, and as I walked into the church my pulse started to race wildly. I knew He wanted something from me that morning, but I was afraid. The electricity of His Presence was all over me, and I could barely focus on what was being said.

Not even the beautiful worship could calm me down, and as the seconds ticked by I felt an insistent pressure to stand up and speak. As I continued to stall for time, the pastor served communion and called for "The Kiss of Peace," which was a five- or ten-minute opportunity to practice forgiveness, reconciliation, or repentance with another believer.

Because of the intense spiritual pressure, I didn't even feel worthy to take communion, yet I kept praying, "Help me, God, and forgive me for being so afraid." Every word spoken in the sermon that morning drove a nail into my heart, and I felt that if I didn't obey God's prompting, I would explode!

After the pastor finished the announcements and everyone was getting ready to leave, I finally leapt out of my seat and said, "Wait! Stop—please! I have to say something!"

Standing there with a dry mouth and a racing pulse, I watched as 250 heads slowly turned and stared right at me. It was now or never.

"I've never really told anyone this, but I can't keep it in anymore," I clumsily blurted out. "I had so much wrong with me, I should be dead now. I had enough injuries to kill ten people, but God healed me. I shouldn't be sitting in this pew—I should be running down the street telling everybody how good He is! I should never stop thanking God for all He's done for me!"

It was anything but eloquent, but it came from my heart. When I finished, I collapsed in exhaustion. The Spirit of God was so intensely upon me, I couldn't stop shaking. No one said a word, and the air was so thick with silence you could hear a pin drop. But then my clumsy words caused many people to praise God.

I'd been standing next to a guy from my home fellowship, and when he quietly reached over and put his arm around me, I burst into tears. As I stood there in his loving embrace, I felt all fear of man melt right out of me.

People came to me from every direction, letting me know how deeply they'd been affected by my words, but I could barely hear what they were saying. There was a powerful sense of purpose coursing through me as I walked out of the church that morning, and when I stepped into the brilliant light of day, I remembered a Scripture,

"So if the Son sets you free, you will be free indeed" (John 8:36 NIV).

I finally understood what that meant. I had just entered through a passageway that would lead me into my personal destiny—my purpose in this life.

Epilogue

Destiny and Beyond

Life is a journey. It is not a random composite of events that fall into meaningless, chronological order. Rather, life is a spiritual pilgrimage with crossroads, bridges, and gateways leading into a pathway of learning to develop our spirit man.

That first stuttering testimony in 1976 released me into a destiny I'd never even dreamed of. Since that day, I've been able to share my story with multiplied thousands of people all over the world.

As I relived my story through the pages of this book, I have come to realize that my life has been like a three-act play. The nineteen years before the crash make up the first act, while the seven years following the accident represent the second act.

Throughout those seven years, God abundantly blessed me with His love, salvation, healing and grace. Though I gladly took what He offered, I was unwilling to give anything in return. Because of my immaturity, the commitment I made to God during those years was weak, erratic, and self-serving.

The third act of my life is composed of all that has happened since that day at Grace Haven in 1976 when I first answered the call of God. I've spoken to juvenile delinquents, devout church-goers, Russian orphans, prisoners on death row, hospital patients, burned-out pastors, people who think they're rich, people who know they're poor, those who worship God and those to whom God is a stranger. In the long run, it really doesn't matter who is in the audience, because my message never changes: Jesus is the Way, the Truth, and the Life.

Blessed Events

Barbara and I continued to flourish at Grace Haven for many months, but because I had an increasing hunger to study the Bible, we eventually migrated to a church that offered deeper teaching. Our little family was still living on the farm, climbing a ladder to get to "poor," but we were so excited about God that we never noticed what we didn't have! I was a walking, talking "Have Bible, Will Travel," willing to go anywhere Jesus would take me.

Our first son, Michael Richard Robinson, was born March 4, 1976. When he was a few months old, we began to notice that he wasn't progressing normally. His head was continually tipped over, and he never tried to get up on his hands and knees in his crib, as we had seen other children do. Our doctor called it "developmental delay," but after four months he had to admit that something was seriously wrong.

After consulting many doctors over the next year, we decided to take Michael to University Hospital in Cleveland for further tests. Strangely enough, the doctors there still couldn't identify his condition. Barbara and I might have been terrified, except that our childlike faith in the Lord overshadowed our fear. We just knew that God was in control, and we treated our son as a normal and beloved child, even though he was not able to stand or walk. By the grace of God, Michael's condition never disheartened us or diminished our forward motion in Christ.

We were now expecting another child, and just before Barbara's due date, we traveled to the Shriners Hospital in Pittsburgh to have Michael tested one more time. When the doctor told us that our son had cerebral palsy, we were devastated, although relieved that there was finally a diagnosis for his condition.

We quickly learned that cerebral palsy is a neurological injury caused by oxygen deprivation either "in utero" or during the process of birth. While our beautiful son's personality was developing on schedule and he was beginning to talk, we were told that he would never walk. Another challenge. Another opportunity for the Lord to show Himself strong!

Just one month after receiving that news, on March 26, 1978, we welcomed into the world our second son—Matthew Robert Robinson—a strong and healthy addition to our growing family. And about that same time, my ministry—one I did not seek—took off.

The Robinson Redemption

Once, when sharing my testimony with some juvenile offenders at the nearby Mohican State Forest Correctional Facility, we saw around ninety hardcore inner city kids, doing time for everything from truancy to murder, come forward to receive Jesus as their Savior. Now I was being asked to speak to some of the inmates at the Mansfield Reformatory, the overcrowded Ohio prison later featured in the movie, *The Shawshank Redemption.* In that shabby facility, while handing out Christian literature to a long line of men, I was suddenly overwhelmed by a supernatural move of God. Something like a "cloud of love" for them descended upon me with such intensity that I could barely stand up. When the chaplain invited me back three weeks later, 400 inmates showed up to hear my testimony, and when I gave the invitation to receive Christ, 55 hardened men came forward, crying. I knew it wasn't me they were responding to. I was merely an instrument of God's love reaching out to these forgotten souls. God hadn't forgotten them, and He had sent me to remind them.

While I was still working odd jobs and scraping together a living for my family, God kept placing me in ministry. Everything seemed to prosper when I put Jesus first and, in the meantime, the Lord daily instructed me concerning the miracle of living by faith. I did what the Lord told me to do, and He took care of my family. As God blessed my ministry, He also blessed us with two more beautiful children—Jacob Ryan Robinson, born on April 10, 1981, and Elizabeth Ann Robinson, born on April 28, 1983.

Soon the whole world literally became my pulpit. After almost ten years of pastoring The Church on Elm Street, I became active in team ministry, spoke at church camps, began networking with other Christian leaders, and conducted training conferences throughout the United States. Doors opened to minister in Europe, Russia, the Pacific Rim, Canada, and Israel. I spoke in schools and orphanages, gave my testimony on Christian radio and network television, and ministered to leaders and pastors from other countries.

In many ways, these past thirty years have simply been a preparation for the glory that is to come, both within the body of Christ and within my own life as a Christian. I believe with all my heart that God has saved His best wine for last!

The Best is Yet to Come

Throughout the years, I've been called a "teacher" or "prophet," but what I am is a messenger. My message is for the broken, the outcast, the wounded, and the oppressed. If God can use me, the weakest of all men, to manifest His love and strength, then there is hope even for the hopeless. The key is: Surrender.

When I was young, I believed in myself and in my own abilities. I worshipped anything that gave me emotional comfort or an adrenalin rush. I spent my time pursuing pleasure, accomplishment, and companionship. But on the day I slipped through this earthly dimension into the heavenly realm, I discovered something that would change me forever; that something was the reality of eternal life. Not until I experienced true brokenness was I willing to admit how much I needed the Lord. I had spent my life energy looking for ways to get my act together. God's not looking for people who've got their act together; He's looking for people who know their act is over!

Maybe you're one of those people who have had an "experience" with God, but have never come into a relationship with Him. Maybe you've even been "born again," but have never chosen to become His disciple. Too many people want God on their own terms—as an insurance policy, a warm fuzzy, a safety net. They kneel to pray, but have no heart to obey. They want Jesus as Savior, but reject Him as Lord. We need to desire Jesus to be the Lord of our lives. Then He will be our Savior, as well.

I know, because I was one of those people. On that freezing morning in Toronto, I finally saw all my selfish choices etched into the pain on Jesus' face and realized that I'd dishonored the most important Person in my life. Yet, even before I surrendered to His lordship, He had been faithful, loving me as a true Father loves his son, despite my rejection of His authority and my abandonment of His protection.

During that seven-year period of time, from the accident in August of 1968 to 1975 when again all was stripped away, I had some serious choices to make. Much of what I thought and believed *was* spiritual truth pertaining to the kingdom of God. In all honesty, however, there was confusion in my life. Our rapidly changing culture was affecting my beliefs, resulting in inconsistent actions in my lifestyle.

Although full of love and genuinely sincere about many things, I was "sincerely wrong" about some very serious issues. The intensely detailed vision I had seen while caught up in the presence of God spanned this seven-year period of future events. Some of the most critical scenes were magnified and resulted in bringing me to a reckoning: Jesus must be Lord of all or not Lord at all. I came from the edge of eternity to the end of myself, to find that you can't have things both ways.

When I cried out, "Give me another chance!" He gave me thirty more years, so far. Like everyone else, I have continued to experience ups and downs, highs and lows. Through it all, I have known His grace.

It's Your Turn Now

The Christian life is not passive or casual. It takes commitment. It takes courage. It takes endurance. I have been backed against many walls, but I have learned that the circumstances don't matter—God is at the center of every circumstance. He walked with me through the Valley of the

Shadow of Death, and He walks with me every day of my life.

I once had a blind eye, but now I can see. I once had a dead leg, but now I can walk. I've heard people say, "If I'd had all those miracles happen to me, I'd be changed, too!" Although those physical healings are an important part of my testimony, nothing is more amazing than the fact that my sins have been forgiven. God healed my body but, most of all, He freed my soul. Miracles won't change you. The change comes when you surrender to His grace.

I believe I would be terribly irresponsible if I did not offer you the single most essential choice anyone will every make. You can pray to God right now and receive His love and power to transform your whole being. Don't worry about the words. They can be as simple as this:

Jesus, I need you. I ask to be forgiven of all my sins. I surrender to You. Help me be a true disciple. I choose to give up my will in exchange for Your will. I want You to be the Lord of my life. Please fill me with Your Holy Spirit and guide me for the rest of my life. I say this in faith, trusting in You, Jesus Christ, my Lord. Amen.

After you have prayed, look up these places in the Bible: Romans, chapter 10, verses 8–10; John, chapter 3, verse 16; Acts, chapter 2, verse 38; John, chapter 17, verse 3. If you need God's help for physical healing, emotional, relational, or financial circumstances, the Lord can help you right now. Then go find some people who are passionately pursuing the Lord in prayer, worship, and relationship with Him and with one another, and hang out with them. Pray together for your city and nation to come into revolutionary revival!

If you have just made the life-changing decision to surrender to Jesus Christ, I hope you'll one day experience something like what I experienced in September of 1994. I was leading a conference at a little church in East Texas. The past two years had been full of painful trials and, to be honest, I was still reeling from the blows.

As I stood in the pulpit that morning, looking out over those people, God spoke something so personally encouraging to me that I began to cry. I was so overwhelmed by His loving approval I could barely stand. As I wept, I had another vision of Jesus.

I had never been able to forget the pain I'd once seen on Jesus' face. I had often thought I couldn't bear to see that look again. In Toronto, I had seen His back turned to me, but on this particular morning He was walking directly toward me. There was a smile on His face that stretched from ear to ear. Though He spoke not a word, the joy in His eyes clearly said to me, "Way to go, Mick! Way to go!"

There is no greater comfort and sense of well being than to know you are pleasing to God and doing what He has destined you to do. If you have just begun your walk with Him, you, too, will learn quickly of His deep, penetrating love for you.

Mickey Robinson
2003, Dawn of the Third Millennium

Just one more thing: Please share this book with others who need to know how much the Lord loves them. Thanks!

Seagate Publications Resources

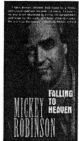

FALLING TO HEAVEN VIDEO
60 minute live video version of Mickey Robinson's testimony. $18.50 | Video (shipping included)

2-Tape Album by Mickey Robinson

Personal testimony/destiny emphasis.
Encouragement: imparting spiritual bravery.
$11.00 (includes shipping)

Strongly Recommended Reading:

$9.00
(includes shipping
& handling)

Holiness, Truth & the Presence of God
by Francis Frangipane

A Penetrating Study of the Human Heart and How God Prepares it for His Glory.

$9.00
(includes shipping
& handling)

The Three Battlegrounds
by Francis Frangipane

An in-depth view of the three areas of spiritual warfare: the mind, the church and the heavenly places.

$9.00
(includes shipping
& handling)

The Stronghold of God
by Francis Frangipane

Finding God's Place of Immunity From Attacks of the Enemy.

For a complete listing of Francis Frangipane's resources & ministry school, please visit www.arrowbookstore.com

Send check or money order to:
Seagate Ministries
P.O. Box 682485
Franklin, TN 37068-2485

Other 2-Tape Albums by Mickey Robinson
· All 2-Tape Albums are 11.00 (shipping included)

Show Me Your Glory
Tape 1: Worship & Intercession
Tape 2: Glory in the Secret Place

Revival Fire! Part One
Tape 1: Waiting to Exhale
Tape 2: The Final Frontier

Activating the Flow of the Holy Spirit
Tape 1: Stirring up the Holy Spirit
Tape 2: Drawing Water from the Well

Revival Fire! Part Two
Tape 1: Strike While the Iron is Hot
Tape 2: Becoming a Fire Carrier

Seagate Publications Resources

Other 2-Tape Albums by Mickey Robinson

All 2-Tape Albums are 11.00 (shipping included)

Can You See The Harvest? Part 1
Tape 1: Being Inconvenienced for God
Tape 2: The Cause

Other resources & itinerary
will be listed at our website
www.mickeyrobinson.com

Can You See The Harvest? Part 2
Tape 1: The Invitation of God
Tape 2: Can You See the Harvest

The Bridge to Breakthrough
Tape 1: Sacrifice and the Release of Power
Tape 2: Sit, Walk and Stand

Prophetic Foundations
Tape 1: The Prophetic Church
Tape 2: Spirit of Revelation & The Release of Faith

Prophetic Initiative
Tape 1: Sharpening Your Prophetic Senses
Tape 2: Prophetic Initiative Part Two

Strongly Recommended Listening:

Jacob's Dream
by Jason Upton
Special! CD - $13.00

Key of David
by Jason Upton
Special! CD - $13.00

Worship
by Michael W. Smith
Special! CD - $13.00

Faith
by Jason Upton
Special! CD - $13.00

Radical Prophetic
Exhortations!!!

Send check or money order to:
Seagate Ministries
P.O. Box 682485
Franklin, TN 37068-2485